Escape From The Hounds Of Hell

by Joseph H. Wachtel

as told to Sylvia Chayat

Escape From the Hounds of Hell

Copyright 1993 by Joseph H. Wachtel

All rights reserved.
Printed in the U.S.A. No part of this book may be used or reproduced in any manner whatsoever without written permission except in the case of brief quotations embodied in critical articles or reviews. Address the publishers for permission to use otherwise, or for information.

Second Edition.

Library of Congress
Cataloging-in-Publication Data

Wachtel, Joseph H., 1914
    Escape From the Hounds of Hell / by Joseph H. Wachtel
        as told to Sylvia Chayat. -- 1st ed.
  p. cm.
ISBN 0-9622584-3-1
1. Wachtel, Joseph H., 1914 -- .
2. Jews -- Ukraine -- Chernovtsy -- Biography
3. Refugees, Jewish -- Soviet Union -- Biography
4. World War, 1939 - 1945 -- Personal narratives, Jewish.
5. Chernovtsy (Ukraine) -- Biography.
        I. Chayat, Sylvia. II. Title.
DS135.U43W33   1993
947' .718 -- dc20
[B]   93-6788
                                                                                    CIP
Library of Congress Catalog Card Number: 93-6788

Published by:
Oceanco Ltd.
6064 Okeechobee Blvd. P.O. Box 170683
West Palm Beach, FL 33417

*In memory of
my beloved wife
Gabriela*

Dedicated to my granddaughters
Natanya and Felice

Acknowledgements

For the realization of this book I want to thank first and foremost Sylvia Chayat for listening and typing all I had to say, and then editing it into a book. I also want to thank the following: Shirley Steinberg, Bill Greenberg, Carol Adler, Will Ray, Dorothy Wilken, Andrew Charlesworth, Pamela Hope-Levin, Judith Levy, Barry Stier, and Susan Morganstein for their advice, guidance, and encouragement throughout the creation of this book.

Foreword

The need amongst Holocaust survivors to tell their story to others has for many become overwhelming in recent years. For some the silence has been kept whilst they built homes and businesses and reared children. For some they had been told to keep silent in the immediate aftermath of the Holocaust; told to 'put all that behind you, people don't want to hear about your sufferings, they've suffered as well', or 'they know about it, they know what happened to you' (when most certainly people had no idea.)

And then forty years later the wall of silence began to break. For some now in retirement with their own grandchildren around them they can reflect on those times when they were part of a family in Europe before 1939, and as they remember, the tragedy of the loss of those families is replayed, perhaps for the first time.

For some those memories had to be told as their survivor friends died, friends with whom they had shared in secret their memories of that horror. With those deaths came the realisation that the number of living witnesses of the Holocaust were diminishing month by month. For certain groups of friends, one of their number had been regarded as the holder of the group's collective memory. Primo Levi was such. With the death of such as these the others might feel impelled to retell the story for fear that it might be lost forever. For each story is different, each story is unique.

For Joseph Wachtel, the need to record his story came when he and his wife, Gabriela retired to Florida. This is the story of Joseph and Gabriela. Within this record of witnessing the Holocaust and resisting Nazism there is also contained a love story.

Yet between planning Joseph's and Gabriela's return trip to Europe and the production of this book, the Stalinist order in eastern Europe had collapsed to reveal, after a few fleeting months of euphoria, old hatreds partially buried for the past fifty years. Joseph and Gabriela's story is so timely. It reminds us of how different peoples and ethnic groups were drawn together by the will to resist Nazi aggression and Nazi genocide. Do we have to be threatened again by malevolent forces such as Nazism to know that we are all brothers and sisters? If so, that is a terrible price to pay. And for the survivors of the Holocaust, if such a price had to be paid it would mean that their witness has been in vain.

Joseph Wachtel has had the courage to retell his story. Let our courage not fail in learning the lesson it teaches us before it is too late.
Andrew Charlesworth
January 1, 1993

Biography of Andrew Charlesworth

Andrew Charlesworth has been on the faculty of the Department of Geography at the University of Liverpool for nineteen years. In 1987 he suddenly found himself being drawn to the topic of the Holocaust. He still finds it difficult to explain how, but he soon became convinced that he as a geographer could make a contribution to Holocaust Studies by taking final year students to Poland to study the landscapes of prewar Jewish settlements and of the Nazi ghettoes and slave labour and death camps. In 1993 he will take students to Poland for the third time. In 1991 he was funded to go on the month-long educators seminar at Yad Vashem. He is now beginning to publish on the geography of the Holocaust.

Additional Notes
by Pamela Hope-Levin
Holocaust researcher and faculty member of Palm Beach Community College, Florida

I took a journey one summer. Elie Wiesel calls it a journey of "fire and ashes." I was memember of a group that dedicated their summer to Holocaust Studies at Yad Vashem. I did enter the kingdom of fire and ashes and learned of the most horrific time in the history of mankind.

But embedded in my memory of this summer was the friendships of my fellow colleagues, a group of dedicated and caring individuals from all parts of the world. One such friend, Andrew Charlesworth, stands out amongst them all. A gentile who so passionately dedicates his life through research and teachings to the study of the Shoah was a guiding light to us all.

Another such friend is Joseph H. Wachtel lives in Lake Worth, Florida. He creates his art work in the local community college. His sculptures have been accepted in Yad Vashem, Jerusalem; the National Museum of the Holocaust in Washington. D.C. and Temple Beth Tikvah in Lake.Worth, Florida. Through his art work he expresses his feelings and memories of the Holocaust.

Andrew Charlesworth the historian and JosephWachtel the witness who lived through it, have entered my lifeo out of the darkness of the Holocaust. Their light is my inspiration.

Prologue

In 1989 my wife Gabriela and I decided to make a trip to Europe to revisit the places where we had fought the Nazis during World War II.

We had planned to go to Hungary, Czechoslavakia, Romania, Austria, and other places which we had helped liberate from the Nazi occupation.

Two things prevented our going; Iraq was getting ready to invade Kuwait and we feared trouble in the area; and also Gabriela was not feeling well.

As it turned out, Gabriela's health deteriorated. We discovered that she had pancreatic cancer. I nursed her until she died in 1991.

In June, 1992 I received two invitations from my sisters in Israel, one for a wedding, the other for a Bar Mitzvah. This double celebration for my sisters' grandchildren could not be ignored and I decided to go to Israel, and then to take the trip to Europe that Gabriela and I had planned.

However by now the Soviet Empire had collapsed. There was no way of knowing whether I would find anything familiar. I called a friend in Budapest who did not encourage me at all. But I decided to go anyway.

I particularly wanted to visit the town of Hatvan, sixty-five kilometers outside of Budapest. During the war the Russians had commanded my unit to erect a monument there to the fallen soldiers. There had been a major battle in Hatvan and many lives had been lost. Our brigade had designed and erected a thirty-five foot tall obelisk built of black granite and marble. We had worked on it almost three months and had been very proud of the result. Now I wanted to see if it was still there.

I flew from Israel to Budapest. My seatmate was a Hungarian Jew. We started talking and I told him my story. He became very interested and offered to drive me to look for the monument. He said he would take me wherever I wanted to go.

Sure enough he picked me up the next morning at the house where I was staying and we started out for Hatvan.

I knew we had erected the monument in front of City Hall in a small park. But everything looked different. It was now summer, and the trees were full of leaves. When we built the monument it was winter. We drove around and nothing was familiar. We asked people and they sent us to a monument which, like so many Russian memorials, had been toppled. But it was not mine. Driving further, all of a sudden, I spotted the black granite of the obelisk. I got shivers over my body. We drove to the site and there it was! Beautiful, gleaming, rising to the sky, like the day it was erected. It was well-tended with flower beds surrounding it.

I walked around it. Forty-seven years after building the monument, all the memories came flooding back.

Chapter 1:
My Home Town

I was born in a little town deep in the Carpathian mountains called Guraputila. It was a Ukrainian area under Austro-Hungarian rule. I was next to the youngest of eight children, four boys and four girls.

The town of Guraputila was nestled in a valley surrounded by high mountains. The roads looked like snakes and followed the rivers. The Christian peasants lived in the higher elevations in the woods as woodcutters and cattle and sheep farmers. The Jews all lived in the town itself, which contained the schoolhouse, the church, the synagogue, a few shops, and the town hall. The town inhabitants, Jews and non-Jews, were poor or lower middle class. There were no wealthy people. Those who were better off moved to the cities. The Jews were tailors, butchers, shoemakers, carpenters, and also dealers in cattle and lumber.

My father was the butcher, the cantor, the shochet, and the mohel. He had a very good education. He had attended the famous Vizhnitsa Yeshiva not far from Guraputila.

When World War I broke out, the Tsarist army attacked our area. The Jews had to flee to avoid Cossack pogroms. My family escaped to a small town in Austria, near Linz, and stayed there for the duration of the war.

My father and mother gathered clothes and food and cooking utensils for the long wagon ride. I was an infant in my mother's arms. The rest of the children rode on top of the household goods and bedclothes. The wagon was pulled by two cows and two horses. The two cows were needed for milk for the family. We traveled in a caravan of many fleeing Jewish families.

The wagon stopped every evening, sometimes in empty army barracks or schoolhouses. Many of the children were coming down with smallpox, dysentery, and other diseases. Austrian army officials were afraid of the spread of diseases to soldiers, so they would raid the encampments and remove sick children and adults for quarantine in sanitation facilities. They were seldom seen again because of the lack of medication and care. The parents began hiding younger children in the chimneys, so that the crying could not be heard. When the children emerged from the chimneys, our parents later told us, we looked like African babies.

After the war we returned to Guraputila. Cossacks had used our homes as stables for their horses. The town was in shambles. The prayerhouse and other buildings were burned down.

The returning families started to rebuild their homes. My father set up the Synagogue in our house, prayers were held there. Teachers were hired for the cheder. Slowly things began returning to normal except that there was no clothing for the children. Most of the material for clothing was made from cloth and linen the peasants wove on home looms. They traded the material for food or services. There was nothing to trade with yet, our mothers were busy trying to make the best out of what we had.

Not having outdoor clothes or shoes for the winter was very harsh and tough. The winter lasted almost six months, from October to March or April. To provide clothing and shoes for our big family of eight children was not easy. During the winter we had to take turns going to school and cheder because of the lack of shoes. Since I was the youngest I could stay out of school and cheder most of the time. Besides this I was blessed with big feet, and the shoes of the other children seldom fit me. During the summer I went to the Ukrainian public school and also to cheder.

Guruputila, the author's sisters and brothers, (l to r) Sarah, Esther, Saul and Mayer

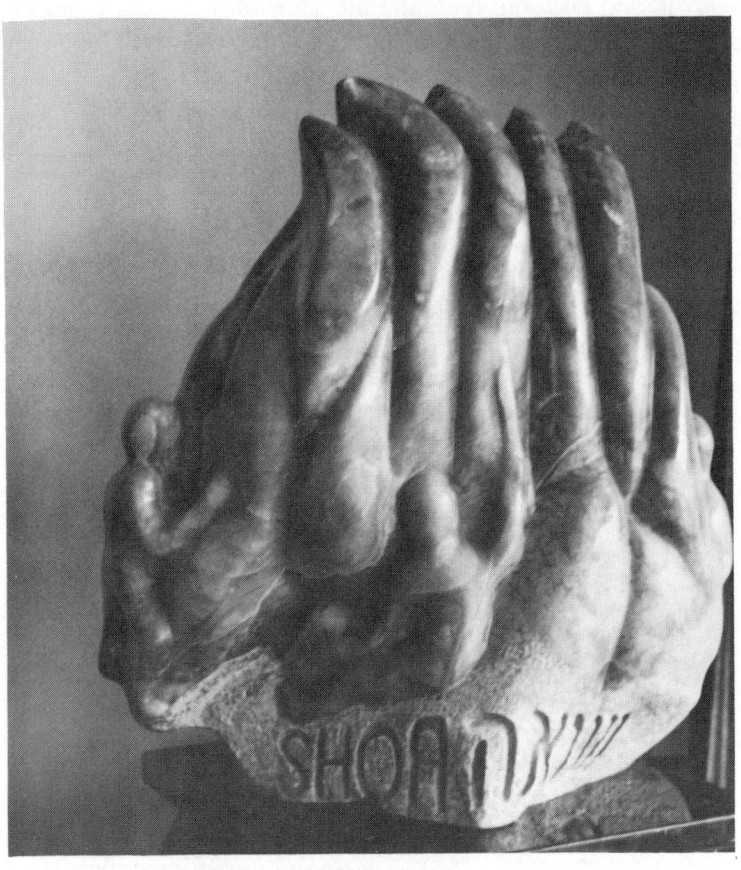

A marble sculpture titled "Shoa" (20 inches high) by the author. This piece honors the heroes & martyrs who fought back against the Nazis. It is on permanent display at Temple Beth Tikvah in Lake Worth, Florida.

Chapter 2:
A Wedding in Town

The wedding of Hannah, Uncle Yankel's daughter, was to take place at the end of the summer. The whole household of Uncle Yankel was in full swing with preparations. I had a crush on Hannah. I was about five or six and she was twenty.

As the days of the wedding came closer, the clothing of every Jew in the town had to be washed and mended and prepared for the event. Shoes were shined, everyone was getting haircuts. The klezmers (Jewish musicians) arrived two days before the wedding night. They came from Vizhnitsa. The cooking had begun a week before the wedding. The children were running around sniffing the air filled with the good smells of roasting chickens, potroasts, cakes and cookies. Almost every house in town cooked something for the wedding.

The musicians started practicing and tuning their instruments. Even the dogs and cats in the village were excited, running around as if they knew that Hannah was getting married.

The day of the wedding arrived. The people in town were bathing and grooming, dressing up and getting ready to meet the groom, who came from another town near ours. The bride was in her parents' home surrounded by friends and family. It was the tradition for a groom who came from another town to be met by young people with decorated horses and wagons and with musicians and drinks. Then they all drove back to the house where the groom was to stay until the wedding. He was not supposed to see the bride before the ceremony.

My family was getting ready for the wedding. Almost everybody was dressed up. At the last minute I discovered that the shoes assigned to me did not fit. I could not pull them on my feet. I had shined them for almost an hour. They were like a mirror. But I could not walk in them. I tried again and again.

With tears in my eyes I went to my mother. She tried to help me, but without results. She sent me to my father. But he could not help. I was told to stay home and later someone would come to see what could be done. It was already time to go to the wedding. My whole family left, and I was alone.

Through the window I saw Leah, a friend of mine, walking with her parents to the wedding. That reminded me that they had gotten a package from America and that in it was a pair of shoes which Leah and I had tried on and that they fit me, were even a little big. I ran after Leah and told her to get the shoes and told her what had happened. It took me a while to convince her. She went back to the house and found the shoes for me, then went back to her parents. She did not tell them anything. After all, we were friends.

I took those shoes, went back home, cleaned them and shined them, and started to put them on. Not bad. They fit. They were lady's shoes: high heels, pointed toes, high uppers, with a lot of shoelace holes. There must have been about twenty-four holes on each side. When I tied the laces the shoes reached my knees. The heels were about three inches high. I pulled them on, tied them up, and tried to walk. I almost fell on my nose. But I did not give up. I figured when it got darker, I could go to the wedding and stay on the side and watch Hannah get married at the chupah.

The wedding was in full swing. The music played, the smell of food and cake was delicious. Children were running around. Uncle Yankel's house was four houses away, not too long a walk, and my dog was next to me all the time. I was afraid of the kids. If they saw me like this on those high heels, I knew I needed my dog.

Finally I got to the wedding. I stood in a corner and one of the boys walked over to me, bent down and looked at my feet. Without saying a word, he ran away. I knew something was going to happen. I stayed in that corner waiting for developments. My oldest brother came over to me and after him, a whole bunch of kids. They stood at a distance in silence. My brother tried to persuade me to go home and not embarrass him and our family. But I just stood silent, not saying a word. Then my father came. He looked at me with a smile. He picked me up in his arms, covered my feet with his caftan (black coat), took me into the main room where all the guests would sit for the wedding meal, put me down on a bench, covered my lap with the table cloth, and said to me, "Sit here until I come back."

Nobody dared to come close to me. My father told my brother to keep an eye on me and tell the kids to stay away. Everybody knew if my father approved what I did, no one could mock me.

The chupah ceremony was over. People started sitting at the tables. My family came too. My father told me not to walk around but to sit at the table and have a good time. My family and friends supplied me with food and drink, including wine.

After a while, I was encouraged to dance in my shoes and became the hit of the party. The news spread that I was dancing in American "shimmy" shoes. My father enjoyed my performance. When Hannah heard about it she came over, picked me up, kissed me, and said, "I love you for what you did. I know it meant so much for you to be at my wedding."

We all had a good time. The wedding was over. I returned the shimmy shoes to Leah. Next day I went barefoot to school and life went on as usual in town.

It was the most beautiful wedding I ever attended.

I am wearing my shimmy shoes J. H. Wachtel

Chapter 3:
The Shoemaker

I was a thumbsucker. By the time I was five or six, my right thumb joint was swollen and irritated by my teeth and there was a wart on it. My parents tried in every way to get me to stop, to no avail.

One day I was sent to bring shoes to be repaired by the town shoemaker, who was not Jewish, but a good friend of the family.

His house had two rooms. In front was the kitchen. The living room was the workshop. I watched the shoemaker and his two helper sons working on shoes. It was fascinating to me. They sat on low stools on a platform and supported the shoe being worked on by a leather belt that held the shoe tight to the knees with the end of the loop around one foot. This was the usual method used by old-time shoemakers.

I sat down in a corner and watched them work on the shoes. I could smell the frying bacon they were having for lunch, a smell that to me was nauseating, because it was not kosher.

The shoemaker's wife called them to the table for lunch. I stayed in my seat. They did not ask me to join them, knowing I could not eat their food. Gradually my thumb went to my mouth as I waited for them to finish eating. I almost fell asleep.

After a few minutes the shoemaker called me to come

over to the table. Startled, I walked over hesitantly. He grabbed my right hand, took out a strip of fried bacon from his plate and rubbed my sucking thumb very, very thoroughly. He said to me, "Now, Yossele, I think you will have to stop sucking your thumb because it is not kosher any more."

My heart almost stopped beating. Frightened, and in shock, I managed to free myself and grabbed my thumb with my other hand. I ran out screaming and crying and ashamed and scared. Children on the street ran after me yelling, "What happened?" Soon a whole pack of children and dogs and grownups were running after me. One told another "He cut his thumb off!" Another said, "We saw blood streaming from his hand!" No one knew what had happened at the shoemaker's.

I ran the mile to our house, and fell into the front room, screaming and crying and shaking.

My father came in and took me on his lap and said, "Now, calm down, my son, tell me what happened to you." In my father's lap I felt secure and I told him what had happened at the shoemaker's.

My father slowly opened my left fist, looked at my thumb, shook his head, saying, "What did they do to you? This is terrible. Now let's see what we can do to fix it." I drank in his words as if they were holy.

He called my mother and said, "Shaindel, bring me a clean rag, a little disinfectant (which he used for circumcisions), and let's wash his thumb thoroughly in warm water."

He cleaned and bandaged my thumb as carefully as if he were performing a circumcision, which I had seen him do many times. He asked my mother for a kerchief and made a sling around my neck to support my hand. He told my mother to wash my face and I was given a glass of milk and a cookie. Father said, "Now don't touch your hand for eight days." When I went to sleep at night he untied the sling and used the kerchief to tie my arm to my body.

After eight days, the bandage and sling came off and I never again sucked my thumb.

Chapter 4:
We Move to Chernovitz

In 1925 my father became sick with pneumonia. There was only one doctor in the whole area. He was not home. My brother traveled twenty to thirty kilometers to find the doctor, but my father died by the time they arrived.

After the death of my father my mother was devastated and heartbroken. She said, "There is no future for us here." She decided to move the family to the nearest big town, Chernovitz where her father and brother lived. Uncle Joshua rented an apartment for us in the outskirts of the town, where the rent was not high. All the children started working. I wasn't even twelve years old, and I was apprenticed to a shopkeeper who dealt in wholesale and retail groceries. I wasn't used to big city life. My grandfather loved me a lot and he took a special interest in me. He bought me clothing and shoes and came almost every day to see me at work. He lived with Uncle Joshua and his family. He was retired and lived on a pension.

He was a good man. He had a beautiful white beard and was very neat. He used to work in a lumber mill and later became the cashier and accountant for the mill. He was a very religious man and at the same time a Socialist. I remember on the first of May he always took me along to parades. He always had a red carnation in his buttonhole and spoke about the struggles of the working people. I did not always understand what he said, but everything meant a lot to me because of his affection for me which I returned.

I did not stay too long at my first job. I had a fight with one of the workers in the store which was more of a warehouse than a store. He teased me, because of my being a mountain boy, and he called me a wild ram. Once he played an ugly trick on me and put me in a very embarrassing situation, for which I never forgave him. I needed to go to the bathroom and did not know where to go. I did not see any outhouse and knew nothing about indoor plumbing. He told me to go into a room in the corner and lock the door from inside and said, "Don't forget to pull the chain hanging from the ceiling." He knew I had never used a flush toilet.

He did not explain to me what it was and what would happen. I went in and followed his instructions. When I pulled the chain, the noise of the flushing water tank, which was high up under the ceiling, scared me so, I jumped forward into the door and hit my nose, which started bleeding. I thought the whole building was falling on my head. I didn't know what to do first, take care of my bleeding nose or pull up my pants. After a while he came looking for me and banged on the door. I did not answer. He called the others. They broke open the door. I was standing there, blood running from my nose, scared to death. I did not know what I had done wrong. I was in pain and I was ashamed. They were all laughing at me. The boss's daughter came over and drove them all off, took me inside the kitchen, washed my face, stopped the bleeding, gave me a glass of milk and a piece of chocolate cake, and calmed me down. I had to tell her the whole story. She was a college student. She took me back to the warehouse and spoke to the manager. He tried to calm me but I was terribly ashamed. When my grandfather came later, I told him I did not want to stay there any more, and I quit my job and left with my grandfather.

Above, Joseph Wachtel in 1938 and Gabriela Farkas a year before we met. Below in California 50 years later.

Chapter 5:
My Teen Years

My next job was in a big wholesale porcelain and glass warehouse. I worked during the day and went to school at night. I worked there about three years. One of my jobs was to deliver purchases made by customers who came for bargains to the warehouse. They tipped me well, which made my mother happy.

I was about fourteen or fifteen when I changed jobs again. This time I started working in a factory which produced knit goods and hosiery. I was assigned by the owner to a German mechanic who came to install knitting machines manufactured in Germany. The machines had to be assembled in our factory for production. This was a good opportunity for me to learn mechanical skills from the German.

The owner of the factory encouraged a group of us to develop and learn thoroughly these new skills. We worked with the Germans over three years and the eight or ten of us became proficient mechanics able to replace the Germans.

By this time I was eighteen and earning good money as an assembly and repair mechanic and was in demand by many factories. I even went to Bucharest, where I worked for two years. I sent as much money home to my mother every week as all the other children put together.

It was now 1935. Economic times were growing bad. I

left Bucharest and returned to Chernovitz and worked in a smaller factory there.

By 1936 the political and economic situation was tense. Eastern Europe was already in the grip of Nazi Germany. The Hungarian Nyilos and the Romanian Iron Guard, both fascist organizations, were strutting around in brown uniforms, similar to the Nazi Storm Troopers, with crossed belts over their uniforms and hand guns at their sides.

Almost all the streets, buses, and trains were full of Nazi-sympathizing volunteers seeking out and harassing Jews. In some cases they were throwing Jews from the speeding trains. I witnessed this once.

One evening a group of my friends were in the public park of Chernovitz. I was working that day on the second shift, from two to ten p.m. I was supposed to join them later in the park.

A group of Iron Guard fascists attacked my friends in the park. One of our girls was grabbed by their leader and held by force. My friends tried to free her and a fight broke out. Suddenly knives and guns appeared and one of my non-Jewish friends, a shoemaker, pulled out his knife, a very sharp cobbler's knife, and threatened to stab the leader of the fascist group if he did not let her go. The leader hit the shoemaker with his free hand, and the shoemaker stabbed and killed him instantly.

The police arrived and arrested most of my friends. In the police station the fascist group came and demanded to be let into the room where my friends were. We don't know exactly what happened but two of my Jewish friends were beaten to death and thrown out of the third-floor window. Later the police gave out a statement that they had committed suicide.

When I came out of the factory at ten p.m. I went to the park. The park was deserted. I felt a tense atmosphere. I heard police whistles. I realized something had happened. I was lucky enough not to meet any policemen, who would have arrested me immediately. I left the park by a back gate and went home. Weeks went by before the trial was set, nobody knew what was going to happen. The shoemaker was given life imprisonment and my other friends were given prison sentences. The fascists got off scot free.

Joseph Wachtel in 1933

Above, Gabriela, (3rd from r.) and the author at her left with friends in Cluj in 1940. Below, Gabriela (l) with members of her family in Cluj.

Chapter 6:
Gabriela

I met Gabriela in May, 1940.

In 1938 it was hard to find work in Chernovitz. I decided to go to Cluj, a city in Romania, where I had friends. I got a job as an assembly mechanic in one of the factories there.

Gabriela came to Cluj to visit friends of hers. It so happened that I knew the same people Gabriela had come to visit. She used to live in Cluj the previous year as a student. I stopped in to visit my friends one day and was introduced to Gabriela. We both felt that something special had happened to us immediately. I had never experienced a feeling like that before.

Meanwhile the political situation started getting worse. It was in August, 1939, when Stalin and Hitler made their infamous pact, which changed the face of Europe.

The Germans annexed part of Poland including Danzig (Gdansk), and part of Czechoslovakia including Sudetenland. The Russians occupied Romanian Bessarabia, half of Romanian Bukovina, and the Carpatho-Ukraine from Czechoslovakia.

Cluj stayed Romanian. The town I came from, Chernovitz, was in Romanian Bukovina, and it became annexed to the Soviet Ukraine. The town Gabriela came from,

Satu-Mare, went to Hungary. All Eastern Europe was in turmoil as borders shut down. The distance between Satu-Mare and Chernovitz was 200 miles. Cluj was midway between the two towns.

Gabriela had come from her Romanian home town of Satu-Mare to visit her friends in Cluj for two days. She stayed almost six days. I was completely taken by her beauty, good manners, good humor, and warm personality. We fell madly in love and talked about getting married.

Gabriela had come from a well-to-do home. Her father had finished college in Vienna. At that time this was possible only for wealthy people. Her mother also came from a rich family of landowners.

Gabriela went home by herself to Satu-Mare to tell her parents about our decision to get married. When Gabriela told them that she was in love, her mother tried to talk her out of it. But she said, "Don't even try, mother. I love him."

After she left I was sorry I didn't go with her, but I had to be at my job. So I never got to meet her parents, because when she returned to Cluj, the situation was very tense. The borders were starting to close down. The Russians announced that all citizens belonging to the Bukovina had two weeks to return there and then the border would be closed.

We called Gabriela's parents for their advice and they said, "Do what is best for you. Save yourselves."

The fascists began to show up on the streets, in the parks, and in everyday life. Arrests, assaults, beatings, confrontations, properties taken away - these were daily affairs in Hungary and Romania.

We decided to choose the lesser danger and go to Chernovitz which the Russians had taken over. We knew that if we stayed in Cluj or Satu-Mare we would be under the Nazis. When Gabriela returned I quit my job and in August, 1940 we left for Chernovitz.

We boarded the train in Cluj. The 150-mile trip was dangerous. There were many stops where everyone had to get off the train. The Iron Guard looted luggage and other property and even ripped watches off people's arms. Often we had to walk many miles along the railroad track hoping another train would pick us up.

Several hundred of us finally arrived at the Russian border in Radautz, exhausted, hungry, filthy. The Romanian border guards marched us like prisoners towards the Russian border which was ten or twenty miles away. There we were met by the Russian border guards who treated us with contempt. They ordered us to go to the railroad station in Siret, the border town. We had to wait there for eight or ten hours. Finally the train to Chernovitz arrived, and we boarded.

 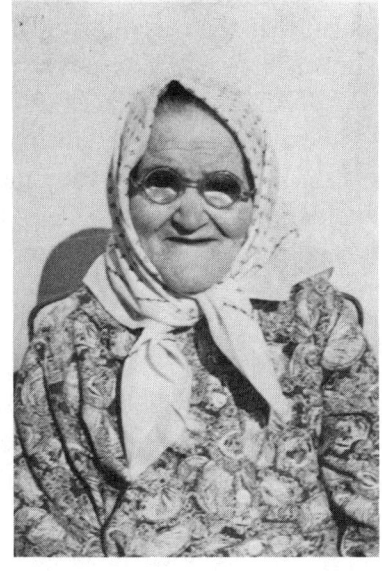

(l-r) Gabriela's mother Pessel and Joseph's mother Shendel.

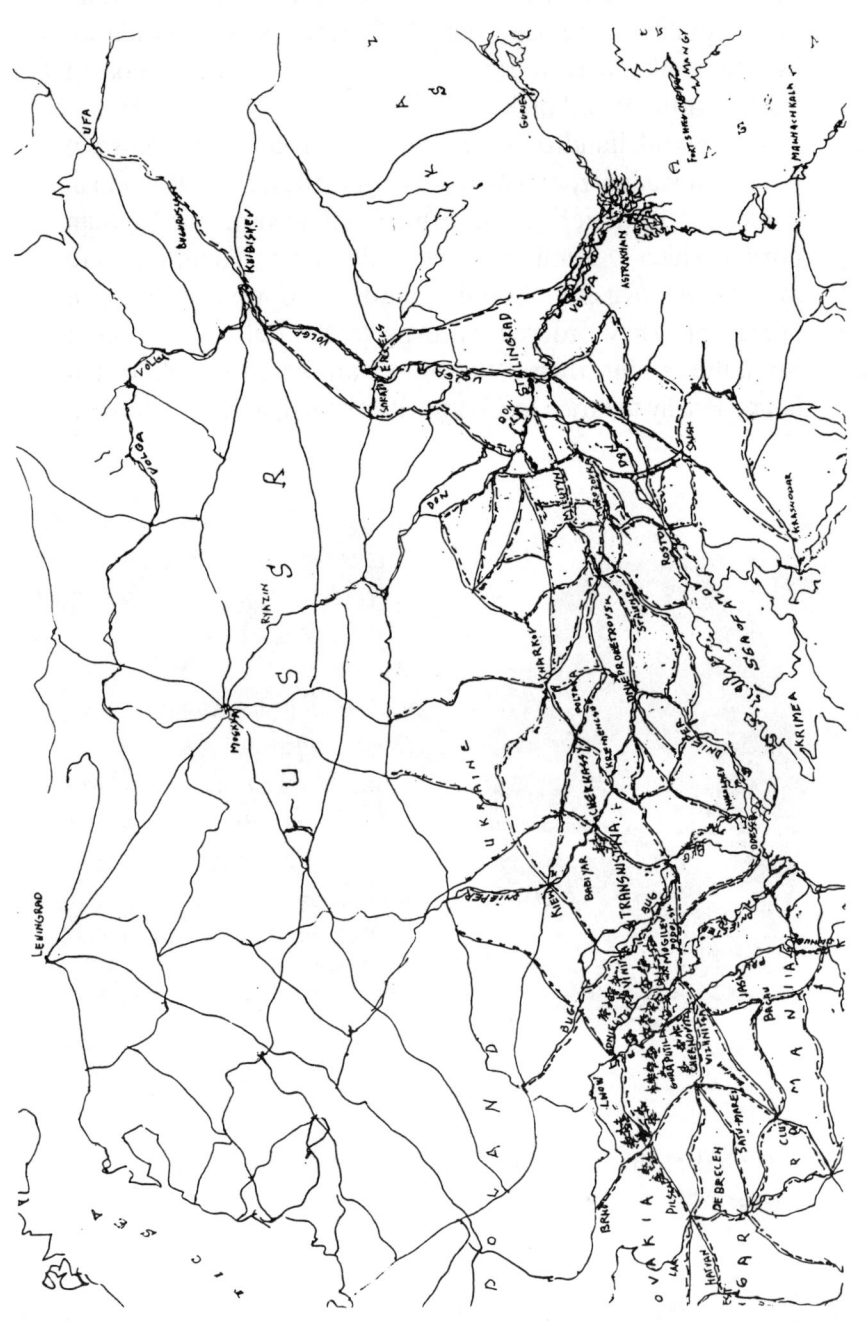

Chapter 7:
In Chernovitz

The first weeks and months in Chernovitz were frightening to the entire population. The N.K.V.D., the Russian secret police, recruited toughs and hooligans not realizing who or what they were. The hooligans arrested merchants, factory owners, and landlords who resisted the nationalization of their businesses and properties mostly Jews.

I did not want to take Gabriela straight to my home. We lived in a poor two-room apartment, without electricity or plumbing. My mother and two sisters lived in one room, and a boarder (my cousin) and I stayed in the other room, which was also the kitchen. Gabriela had come from a relatively wealthy home with big rooms, high windows, and beautiful furniture. I wasn't sure how she would react, so I took her to my brother Sol's house. He and his wife, Eda, had a nice little apartment in the city, and Gabriela stayed with them.

The next day I took her to be introduced to my mother and sisters as my future wife. My mother was so impressed with Gabriela. Although she was half-blind with cataracts, she insisted that Gabriela move in with us. My mother said to her, "You are now my child too," and we all cried.

Gabriela moved in with us. We both found jobs. Under the Russians all the businesses were nationalized. It was easier for strangers without connections to the former business owners to find work. Gabriela became manager of a cosmetics and drug store. I got a job at City Hall in the Building & Housing Department.

My mother was happy to prepare food for us and to take care of the house. And so we lived together for almost two months. Gabriela loved my mother very much. My mother was an intelligent woman and she made Gabriela feel like her own child. She said to Gabriela, "I will be your mother until you are reunited with your own mother."

One day Mother said, "Children, we have to think of getting the youngsters settled." My younger sister Pepi also had a boy friend. Mother said, "Let's make one wedding for the two couples."

And so it was decided. We registered officially in City Hall as married couples. The Russians did not permit religious weddings. We also set a date for a secret religious home wedding. We needed a rabbi. A neighbor who was a religious man conducted the ceremony. This was strictly for the family, about ten or twelve people. The canopy or "chupa" used in the ceremony was a big tallis which had belonged to my father. We used four sticks to raise the tallis but had to be careful because the ceiling was low.

Now the two young couples had to look for apartments, which were almost impossible to find. We were able to rent furnished rooms in the city.

There was no mail connection to Satu-Mare in Hungary, so Gabriela could not let her parents know that she was getting married. We did not know until after the war that Gabriela's mother was taken to Auschwitz. After the war we found one person who survived and had been with her in Auschwitz until she was taken to the gas chamber. Her father disappeared without a trace.

Chapter 8:
With the Partisans

On June 22, 1941, about six in the morning, the sirens started wailing in Chernovitz. We had no radio or telephone and to find out what was happening we ran out to the street. We heard cannons and saw planes bombarding the outskirts of the city.

The Nazis attacked the region by surprise. Little resistance was shown by the Russian army and they started to retreat in panic.

The Germans had organized Nazi sympathizers and had instructed and ordered them to do their bidding when Chernovitz was attacked. The neo-Nazis took over City Hall. The city authorities, who were Russians, fled east. The new city officials were composed of the worst elements of the city. They set up ghettos in the city surrounded with barbed wire. They formed civilian police units. Using loudspeakers, they ordered all Jews into the ghettos. There were two separate ghettos in Chernovitz.

Those who did not obey were beaten and dragged into the ghettos or killed. My mother and sister happened to live in an apartment in one ghetto area. Gabriela and I went to my mother's apartment and soon there were about thirty people crammed into the two rooms.

The Germans had not yet taken over Chernovitz. The

Russians had trucks that were supposed to evacuate the people, but the party officials and factory directors commandeered most of the trucks for their own families and household goods, leaving those who wanted to leave stranded, mostly Jews.

Those of us who were able-bodied were rounded up daily from the ghetto for various jobs. Gabriela was assigned to take care of the children and the sick. Because Gabriela tried to protect her patients from selections, the Nazi collaborators hit her on the back with the butt of their guns. This broke a bone in her spine. She did not realize what happened but kept on working with pain, afraid to be selected with the sick.

As the Russians retreated from Chernovitz they gave orders for all citizens wanting to flee the city to assemble at City Hall where trucks would be waiting to evacuate them. Gabriela was at City Hall and got on a truck that was supposed to pick me up along with the rest of my family. But the Russian driver went for his own family instead. My sister Sarah spotted Gabriela on the truck and yelled her name. Because battles were now taking place in the streets, Gabriela was afraid to jump off the truck which had picked up speed trying to get out of the city.

Meanwhile the war was coming closer and the truck stayed on the road trying to outrun the battles. The truck driver finally dropped Gabriela and her friend Sonya in a camp in the Transnistria area. Transnistria means the area across the Dniester River. There were already 1500 other Jewish people, mostly from Poland, at the camp.

I was on a job assignment and did not know that Gabriela had boarded a truck. When she did not return home that night I nearly went crazy. There was curfew and I could not go out looking for her. My oldest sister Sarah said she was sure she had seen her on a truck with other people. My only hope was that she was safe somewhere, but how to find her? And so we lost each other!

After about two months, selections started in the ghettos for transport to the concentration camps. Families were separated from each other. Some of my brothers and sisters and I were shipped to Mogilev Podolsk camp, about a hundred kilometers away. Others of my family went to Bershad. We knew nothing about each other. I was devastated.

In the beginning the camp supervision was chaotic. The Nazis did not have enough guards until they began training Ukrainian collaborators. A rumor spread through the camp that those who wanted to should try to escape and join the partisans in the nearby woods. I hoped this would enable me to find my wife.

One night about thirty of us escaped. We went through the barbed wire in small groups. The first group silenced the guard and it took the rest of us two to three hours to get past the barbed wire. We ran to the woods and found them full of people -- Russians, Jews and refugees from all over. We slept on the ground and ate whatever we had with us. I searched for my wife with no results.

The Jewish people kept together. A brigade of 150 to 200 was formed, led by Vassily Yonovich. The brigade was split into platoons of ten or twenty. Many of us had belonged to Zionist youth groups, similar to the Boy Scouts, and we knew the importance of discipline.

When we could we built zimlyankas, underground shelters that protected us from the weather. We could keep warm by making makeshift stoves out of tin. As many as ten or twelve people could stay in a zimlyanka. Boards and branches acted as camouflage for our roof. Leaves and branches on the dirt floor were our mattresses. We tried to dig them against hillsides or under heavy tree roots. It took four or five hours to make a zimlyanka.

By the time we joined the resistance in the wooded area constant fighting was taking place. It wasn't a real front, but a series of skirmishes. We had to fight for survival. The

Russian army was in disarray and retreating in panic. They paid very little attention to us. I remember where we tried to tell the Russians that we were Jews, but that made things worse, because they were afraid to be caught with us by the Nazis. In some instances complaints were heard from our boys who said, "Why did we have to leave? We should have stayed with our families. If we have to die we should die together."

To keep morale high, scouts were sent into towns to find out about the front line, about the whereabouts of the enemy, about food supplies in collective farms. The scouts returned with enthusiastic reports about how to evade the enemy or about cabbage or potato fields we could make use of.

In many places we came across local Russians digging anti-tank trenches. These trenches were about twenty feet deep, with sloping sides, covering the countryside in zig-zag formation, for miles and miles. This was to trap the Nazi tanks and stop their advance. The orders for doing this came from the Russian high military command. The trenches were dug at night and camouflaged during the day because of the Nazi reconnaissance planes that bombed anything suspicious.

The work was done by hand by the local population digging with picks and shovels. It was done grudgingly. Some of the Ukrainians would have welcomed the Nazis. They were unhappy with the Bolshevik regime which had nationalized their farms and sent their landowning parents to Siberia during Stalin's collectivization period.

This was all being done behind the front lines. As we arrived in those areas, we volunteered to work on the tank traps. This enabled us to get food from the farms, and it enhanced our reputation for future projects for the Russian Army, it also kept us alive.

One night we were camped on one side of the Dnieper River and could hear the Nazis singing and talking on the other bank. Suddenly we heard the creak of oars. Two rowboats were being rowed to our side. Four men landed on our shore. We let them come up the bank. They never returned to the Nazi camp. The next day the Nazis apparently were ordered to move out, because they never investigated the loss of the four Germans.

The tank traps were never used. The Nazis broke through in other areas.

Meanwhile Gabriela had also escaped with a group of people from her camp. As soon as they reached a Russian army unit, the Russians stopped them and took them deeper into the country, away from the front lines, to put them to work on collective farms and also for safety from the Nazis. They worked in different jobs in order to maintain themselves and to survive. When the front line came too close they were always moved deeper into Russia. Her group was now in Milutyn, on a collective farm near Rostov. Gabriela was assigned to a medical center.

Signs were now being posted in all the refugee camps that those who wanted to locate family members should register with the main refugee center office in Buguruslan. Buguruslan was located in central Russia, far from the front. The refugee center was set up to reunite families split up by the war. Gabriela sent in her name and location.

One day the front came so close to where they were that they had to be moved out. They were transported to Stalingrad on trucks and trains. From there they were shipped by boat down the Volga to Astrakhan and then over the Caspian Sea to Kazakhstan in middle Asia where the Russians needed laborers for canning factories, coal mines, and other industries.

Meanwhile as partisans, we had no permanent mailing address because we were constantly moving around. The Nazis would move in and we would move out. In order to maintain contact, I always gave as my mailing address the post office where I thought I might be able to be contacted. I studied the map and tried to figure where Gabriela might be at that time, if she were still alive. I wrote letters daily and sent them to Buguruslan, hoping to get an answer.

Joining the resistance in the Vinitza woods, Ukraine 1941

Chapter 9:
Contact is Made

For eight months we did not know if either one of us was still alive.

On March 8, 1942, I got an answer from Buguruslan that my wife Gabriela was in the town of Milutyn near Rostov and that she was working in a medical center on a collective farm . This was about forty kilometers from the place where I was at that time, in the town of Morosovka.

Upon receiving this news, I almost went crazy. Excited, I ran around with the letter in my hands, showing it to everybody and planned with my friends how to reach her. It was decided to have somebody go with me to find her and bring her back into our unit.

I got a horse-driven sleigh, there was still snow on the ground and, with my friend, drove an hour or more at top speed. The horses were soaking wet. Arriving at Milutyn, we went straight to the medical center after being given directions by the local people. It was late in the afternoon. The center was already closed. Only a cleaning woman worked there. We went in and asked for Gabriela. The woman was very scared at seeing two excited strangers with guns demanding to see Gabriela, the refugee.

I tried to explain to her, but she did not seem to understand. After looking at me for a few minutes she then recognized me from the picture Gabriela had once shown her. She did not want to tell me that Gabriela was no longer in Milutyn, that she had been evacuated together with all the other refugees when the front line came closer.

The cleaning woman ran away to tell Asya, a young lady dentist from Rostov, who had been Gabriela's roommate and close friend, and to tell her that Gabriela's husband was here. I ran after her to the building. Asya came out, and seeing me, she also recognized me from the pictures. She was so excited. After calming down, she invited us in, asking questions, and telling me that Gabriela had left Milutyn several months ago. She had just gotten a letter from Gabriela a few days ago from Kazakhstan where she was working in a coal mine.

She showed me the letter. I took the letter with shaky hands and I started to read. I felt great joy just to see her handwriting! Gabriela described to Asya details of her journey to Mangyshlak in middle Asia on the other side of the Caspian Sea. How they traveled down from Stalingrad to Astrakhan by boat on the Volga River, then on big ships to cross the Caspian Sea. The journey took two to three days. From there they went deeper inland to Mangyshlak where the coal mines were. They were placed in wooden barracks and assigned to work in coal mines, kitchens, and other work places. Gabriela described that she was very heartbroken. She said she wished she had never left Asya. The climate and working conditions were harsh. She was in an entirely new world - a world of desert, sand, heat and wind.

After reading this letter I began bombarding Kazakhstan with telegrams and letters when ever I could find a functioning Post Office.

Chapter 10:
Gabriela in Kazakhstan

I later learned more of Gabriela's journey to Kazakhstan. On Gabriela's route from Stalingrad to Astrakhan, while traveling down the Volga River, all the people on the ship came on deck to get a little sun and stretch out. They were tired of sitting in the cabins. All of a sudden an air raid alarm was sounded. An enemy airplane had broken through the defense lines, and was dropping bombs around the ship.

Meanwhile one of the women started giving birth on the deck. All the passengers ran for shelter below, leaving her there. Gabriela remained on deck with the woman, who was screaming in pain, giving birth. She did not leave her, but assisted her through the ordeal. It was a girl and they named her Victoria, for Victory.

When the ship docked in Astrakhan, they were transferred to a bigger boat which took them over the Caspian Sea to Fort Shevchenko and then to the coal mines of Mangyshlak.

About 1500 people had come over with that transport from Astrakhan. Everybody was put to work. They were placed in temporary barracks. Gabriela and a group of people were put to work in a coal mine.

The climate in the region was terrible. It was a desert, with hot winds that choked the breath and sandstorms that blinded the eyes. Not a tree or a leaf was to be seen. Nothing grew there. Milk was gotten only from camels. Other food was scarce. There were goats and sheep that grazed on the cactus plants. The winds there are called *buran* and are so strong they stir up big funnels of sand and dust. It is impossible to see, breathe, or walk. One must take shelter during a buran.

Soon after they arrived, many of the refugees fell sick with typhus, scurvy, and other sicknesses. Gabriela got typhus and was very sick. They took her to a hospital in Fort Shevchenko, where she remained for almost two months. Then she went back to the coal mines of Mangyshlak and worked there for almost a year, not knowing, of course, where I was or even if I was still alive. Her only hope was to be reunited with me one day.

Gabriela later also came down with scurvy which was the main killer amongst the refugees when it reached the stage of despair. She was put out into the hallway because she was not expected to live. Scurvy has a bad smell from the open wounds and pus. Of the 1500 refugees, mostly Jews from Poland and Ukraine, sent from Astrakhan to Mangyshlak, about 1200 did not survive.

By some miracle one of my telegrams did get through and was read to her by her roommates and friends. When she realized I was alive and coming for her, she had such a strong will to live that she sat up in her bed in the hallway. She said, "If he's alive, I must live, too!" From that moment on she started to get stronger and stronger. She asked for all kinds of things that would help her gain strength. She implored from her friends to help get medication and food, -- onions, cabbage, leftovers, -- whatever they could give her. Day by day she got better. Her friends took her back into their room and she started to walk around a little bit at a time. After a few weeks she asked to be assigned to work. She was assigned to a medical laboratory in the local hospital, which had ten or fifteen beds. Working there she became friends with a young lady doctor, Salima Abatova, and received better treatment.

She showed Salima the letters from me, told her that I was a freedom fighter somewhere near Stalingrad and that I would come for her someday. She said to Salima, "I have to live to see him. Please help me, Salima." And Salima did help.

She began answering my letters. The mail was very unstable, so I got letters every two to four months in different towns. I had instructed her where to send the letters. Gabriela received my mail now and then. But the main thing was that we were in contact, that I knew where she was and that we both knew the other was alive.

The author in the Soviet Union, 1942

Battles in Stalingrad, Winter 1942-43 J. H. Wachtel

Chapter 11:
The Battle of Stalingrad

As the war intensified the Nazis penetrated deeper into the Soviet Union. We got to be more involved. We were moved around to different front lines. In Rostov we boarded big boats on the River Don. Our destination was Stalingrad. There was a general order sending everybody and all material to Stalingrad. The enemy had to be stopped. Both the Russians and the Nazis concentrated their full strength on that front.

And so we were shipped down the Don River to port cities near Stalingrad where we landed. We took up positions for the defense of the region. Our unit was assigned to a pontoon engineering brigade. It was winter, 1942, a harsh, cold winter. Stalingrad was still free. We were in and out of the city for all kinds of missions - tools, materials, and supplies.

The city was already under enemy bombardment. Defense positions had to be built in different parts of the city, especially on the banks of the Volga River.

The Russian strategy was to cut off the Nazi forces which had advanced to the city in a wedge formation. The Russian army's aim was to encircle the enemy inside the city. This they accomplished and the German army's backbone was broken.

There were tremendous losses on both sides.

Our brigade was called on wherever there was a weak spot in the encirclement. The Russians thrust guns in our hands and sent us off to fight. Even the cooks and the wounded were used for first line duty.

Stalingrad is a big city about 20-25 Klm. along the Volga River and had a lot of industries. A big tractor factory, one of the biggest in the Soviet Union, and other heavy industries. The defense of Stalingrad was based on defense lines built on the River banks, trenches were dug in deep along the Volga banks underground fortresses. Almost all the population was engaged in construction of the defense of the city. We worked in shifts 24 hours a day under the most stressful horrible conditions. After rain mud was up to the knees, trucks had to be pushed by hand, digging them out of the mud was very common. Almost every truck loaded with tools and material was stuck in the mud. Driving in and out of the city was very dangerous. Occasionally the Nazis broke through the air defenses and dived down to the roads. Almost every moving object was fired upon with machine guns, and the planes turned around 2-3 times, firing even on single individuals.

After the big battles of Stalingrad and heavy fighting ended, the Nazis were driven and pushed back out of the city. It was the turning point in the war for us. This was the end of our partisan activities and we were incorporated in the construction Brigades to restore roads and bridges.

Chapter 12:
The Reunion

During the battles of Stalingrad, in the winter of 1942-43, on February 25th I was wounded in my left leg. My wound was not that bad -- I could move around with a crutch. I asked my commander, Vassily Yonovich, if I could go on leave instead of going into a hospital. The fighting was very heavy and the Russians were pushing the Nazis back from Stalingrad. He said to me, "Are you sure you can do it in your condition? The going will be hard. It's a long distance, and even if you find her, how will you get back to us? And will they permit her to leave?" But seeing my determination, the brigade leaders agreed to let me go. They gave me a nice letter of recommendation that said I was wounded and on leave. That I was going to pick up my wife, who was in danger of her life, and to bring her into our unit.

My friends gave me food, money and prayers. I boarded a freight train south to Astrakhan in March, 1943. I knew exactly the route which she had described in her letters. The Volga was still frozen, so ships could not go into the Caspian Sea, I had to wait in Astrakhan until the Volga became navigable.

When I arrived at the station in Astrakhan, I went looking for a place to stay. Across from the railroad station there were apartment houses. A young boy was standing there in front of one of the buildings. I went over to him to ask about lodging. The boy was around fifteen or sixteen. His name was Kim. We took to each other right away. Seeing me limping with a crutch, he invited me into his home. I asked him with whom he lived. He said, "With my mother." I asked, "Where is your mother now?" He answered, "In the bakery, where she works." I later found out that she was the director of a big bread factory, and that he also had an older brother who was in the army. His father had died many years ago.

The boy said to me, "Joseph, wait here. I'm going to telephone my mother that you are here, because if I let you go without telling her she might be mad at me. Please wait."

He called his mother on the phone and told her there was a wounded soldier at the house and he wanted to help wash his wound and make him comfortable. She said, "Don't let him go. Tell him to wait there. I will be home soon."

After about half an hour she walked in and introduced herself. "I am Valentina Petrovna, the mother of Kim. What is your name?" I said, "I am Josef Israelovich." I told her how I came to Astrakhan and what my mission was. She told me to not even think of going away and looking for another place to stay. Kim had a room that he had shared with his brother who was now in the army and they were more than happy to have me there for the time I had to spend in Astrakhan. She might even be able to help me to get across the Caspian Sea. She was a very influential person in the city of Astrakhan.

I was there for almost ten days. She contacted her friends. One of her friends was the secretary of the Commander of the Caspian Sea flotilla, General Loginoff. The secretary invited us one evening to come over to her house. She lived with her mother, who had been an opera singer, a beautiful elderly lady, now in her seventies. We had coffee. I had to tell them my story, and the mother said to her daughter, "You have to help these two young people." They were all very supportive. To Valentina Petrovna I was already a family member. The secretary said she would speak to the Commander and would let us know.

After a few days we got a phone call from the secretary asking me to present myself to the Commander's office packed and ready to leave. Kim came with me. After a wait I went in to meet the Commander. He summoned a Captain who took me to a cargo plane which shipped cans to the fish canneries on the other side of the Caspian Sea, in Kazakhstan. We flew over the Caspian Sea and landed in Fort Shevchenko in only three to four hours.

A truck took me from the airport to town and I went straight to the hospital of Fort Shevchenko where I knew Gabriela had been when she had typhus. I hoped to find more information there. Mangyshlak, the town where she lived now was about 100 kilometers inland and I figured they would tell me at the hospital how to get there. I also needed medical attention for my wounded leg.

The people in the hospital were very cooperative and helpful and even excited at the appearance of someone wounded at the front. The staff of the hospital was almost all women. The head doctor remembered Gabriela well and she tried very hard to help me. She put me in touch with the postmaster who delivered mail to the surrounding communities by camel and horse-driven wagons. The postmaster promised to include me in a caravan of camels leaving the next day. In the meantime I was to stay in the hospital overnight.

Later the chief doctor called me in to let me know that a truck was leaving early in the morning to pick up coal from the coal mines in Mangyshlak. This would be faster than the two-day trip with camels.

The next morning we left for Mangyshlak. We drove four to five hours over difficult terrain on roads marked with straw-topped poles ten to twelve-feet high, to show the way. The poles were needed because the wind-driven sands blocked and blotted out the road in some areas. We arrived in Mangyshlak. The truck driver took me straight to the hospital building.

I invited the driver to meet us later to be introduced to Gabriela. He too, was excited at our reunion. The driver left, and I went into the hospital. Gabriela was not there. She had left for the barracks in which she lived with a group of people.

One of the nurses recognized me from Gabriela's picture of me. She ran to show me where the barracks were. She wanted to be the one to bring the news. She was faster than I was. I couldn't keep up with her. When I reached the barracks she came out with a group of screaming people. "Gabriela's husband is here!"

But Gabriela was not home! She was at a neighbor's house knitting with them. They were making shawls out of camel's hair for each other, because the nights were cold.

Her friends at her barracks invited me in and made me wait there. They were afraid she was still too weak to take the shock of suddenly seeing me, although she knew I would come some day.

So they decided to send somebody to tell her that she was needed in the hospital. They knew she would have to go home to put on her uniform.

I could not sit in the room any more. I came out into the very long hallway as she entered the other end. I saw her and started walking toward her, trembling. She began walking faster. As we came closer she began running and I started running towards her. As soon as we reached one another she fainted. She did not say one word or make a sound; she just collapsed into my arms.

We cried a lot. She just lifted her head, looked into my eyes, and fainted again. With the help of her friends we got her into the room she shared with three other women.

We just looked at each other. We said not one word. We tried to take deep breaths to calm down. It took a long time. People brought us water. We sat on the edge of her bed just looking and touching each other, still not able to talk.

We vowed that never again would we be separated.

Chapter 13:
In Kazakhstan

Our reunion shook us. We sat on her bed, held hands, and tried to talk. She was so very frail. I was almost afraid to touch her. I told her what I had gone through during our separation.

Gabriela drank in my words, then said, "How happy I was when I learned you were alive! I knew you would come to save me, because if you did not come, I was going to die. In my sleepless nights I used to plan our future together. And now that you are here it's hard to realize it isn't a dream."

I stayed there six to eight days. Two days after my arrival, Gabriela took me around the town of Mangyshlak. She took me to the marketplace, to a few shops, to City Hall -- I accompanied her on all her errands. The shops had hardly any merchandise. There was almost no stock on the shelves.

The marketplace was the most interesting place to visit. The peasants from the surrounding villages came with small amounts of produce -- eggs, goat milk, camel milk, yogurt made from those milks, camel and sheep wool. They sold their goods for money and also traded with each other. There were a few covered sheds for protection from the strong sun. It was colorful, like a flea market.

By this time I was rested and we started making plans to leave the area. But we were told by good friends of ours to

KAZAKHSTAN MANGISHLAK VISITING FRIENDS FOR DINNER EATING DISH BARMACK APRIL 1943

keep very quiet and low-key about our departure because Gabriela had become important in the hospital where she worked. She was treating one of the police chiefs whose life she had saved. As a nurse she had kept him from bleeding to death until the doctor arrived. He considered her his savior and he had the power to keep her from leaving town.

Local people and friends had begun inviting us to their homes. My arrival in Mangyshlak was a major event. I was someone wounded at the front lines where the war was going on. Everybody wanted to hear first hand about the war, especially when they learned I had been in the Stalingrad area, which was the turning point of the whole war.

One evening we were invited to the home of one of the local Kazakh families, a Mongolian slant-eyed people. The man was an important city official. Everyone there was sitting on the floor on a mat with a cushion to lean on. Shoes were left at the entrance of the apartment. There were no chairs or tables. The center of the floor was empty but covered with a round cloth about forty inches across. It held a few bottles of vodka and other drinks. We were invited to sit down and were offered drinks. Almost everyone sat yoga-style, with crossed legs. I could not do it because of my wounded leg, so I had to sit sideways with my leg extended.

One of the guests played the dumbra. It is a banjo-like instrument with a very long neck, about 35-40 inches long, with two strings. It had a monotone sound. The people were singing along with it. We had a good time. Of course I didn't know the songs, but Gabriela knew some of them.

The hostess and her friends were busy preparing supper. Until then we had little snacks like goat cheese or camel cheese. Then the hostess announced that supper was ready. A big bowl was placed in the middle of the cloth on the floor-table. The hostess poured the food, called bishbarmak, into the bowl. This was lamb meat and dumplings mixed together in a sauce. The soup made from the boiling meat was passed around in a smaller bowl from hand to hand, and everyone took a sip from the bowl.

Everyone was now invited to eat. There were no utensils, but we used our hands to dip into the large bowl. This is called "eating bishbarmak" - eating with five fingers. When I tried it, the food ran down my arm. The others ate delicately without any problems. We had a lot of fun, with everyone trying to teach me how to eat with five fingers. Even the children came over to try to teach me. A sip of vodka from a glass was much easier.

After supper came the big attraction. The "table" was cleaned up and the hostess came over with the big shank bone of the lamb nicely cleaned off with a towel. It was handed over to the host and he took it in his hands. The tradition is that he or somebody who is a special guest is invited to break that shank bone in two with one blow of the fist. The towel could be used as a cushion on top of the bone to protect the hand. Being a special guest from far away, I was offered the honor.

Everyone tried to talk the host out of offering it to me, but I took a chance. I felt if I could get through all that had happened to me I could break that bone. Also I had been trained in hand-to-hand fighting as a Resistance fighter. I laid that bone in front of me, placed the towel on top of it the way they instructed me, and with one blow I broke that bone in two. There was great silence in the room. The people looked at each other in wonder and said I must be a real Kazakh, that my eyes were even a little slanted. There was a big celebration and we had a good time until the party was over.

During the next few days I was awaiting the truck driver who had brought me to Mangyshlak. I had arranged with him, that when he came back for another shipment of coal in approximately eight days, to contact me. He finally came. We did not tell anybody about our plan, that Gabriela and I were preparing to leave with him to go to Fort Shevchenko and from there to sail over the Caspian Sea to Astrakhan.

We asked the driver to leave in the middle of the night, so as not to awaken suspicion. Arriving in Fort Shevchenko

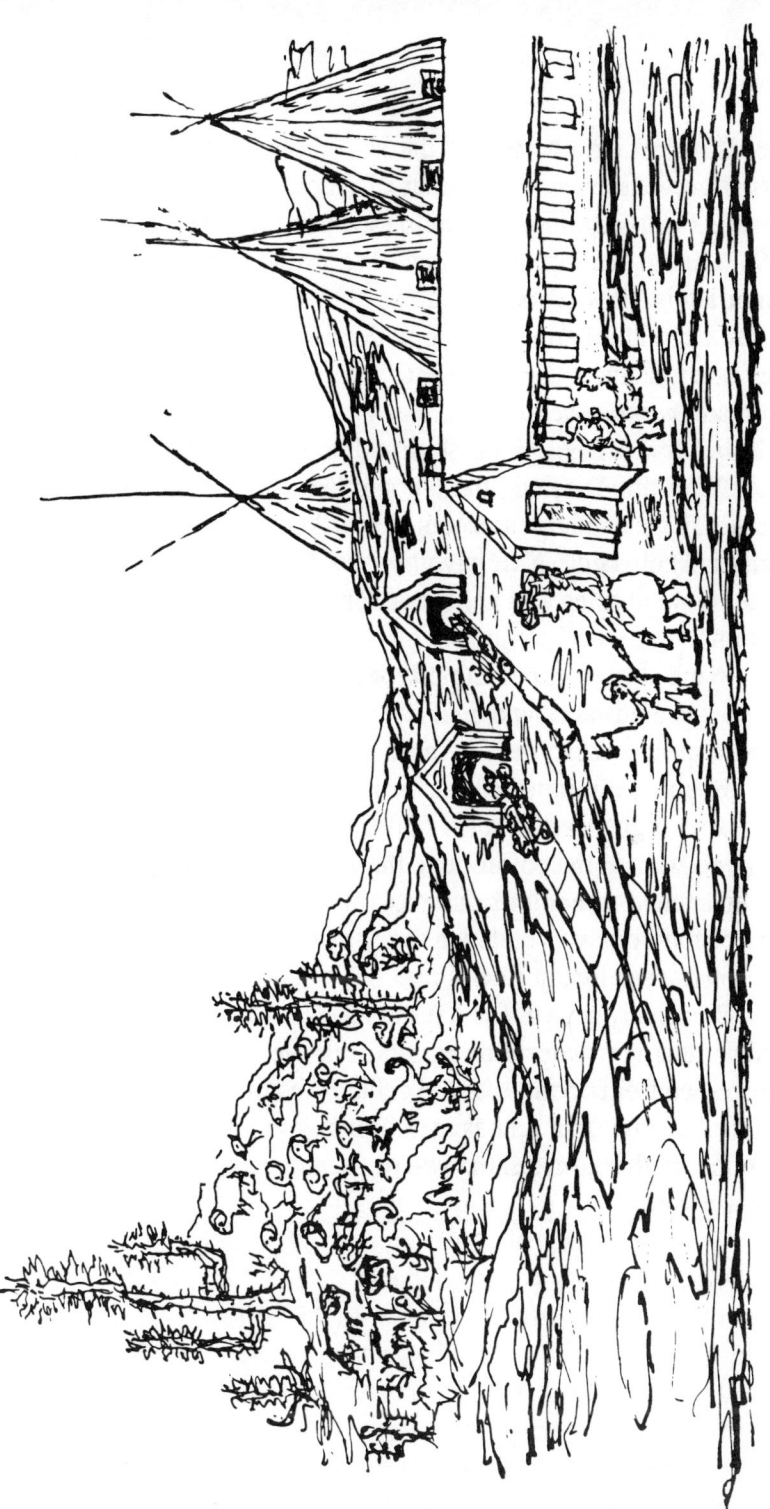

Spring 1943, coal mine in the desert of Mangishlag   J. H. Wachtel

we drove straight to one of the ships. The Commander in Astrakhan had given me a letter of recommendation to the captain of that ship. It was early in the morning. The sailor on watch went to get the captain. After I showed him my letter he immediately took us on board the ship. I explained to him briefly what had happened. He understood and said, "Don't you worry. I am responsible for you." He assigned us to a cabin and we felt secure.

In a few hours a Mangyshlak police patrol on horseback hailed the ship. They could not board because the gangplank was up. The captain came out. He asked them what they wanted. They said, "You have two people on board, a man with a wounded leg and a woman. They have to come back with us."

We had been expecting this to happen.

The captain answered, "I have an order from my Commander in Astrakhan to take these two people on board and they are under my jurisdiction. I am responsible for them."

They argued for a while and then turned around and left.

We were in the port for two days and were able to watch the fish canning operations that took place on the ship. It was a lot of fun and everybody was very nice to us. The delta of the Volga was already free of ice.

We finally set sail for Astrakhan. The Caspian Sea was very rough. We were both seasick, but we didn't care. We were tossed from one side of the deck to the other, but it was still fun. We became real sailors. When you are in the early twenties, nothing matters if you're together and happy, the way we were.

Chapter 14:
In Astrakhan

After sailing across the Caspian Sea we arrived in Astrakhan. We said good-bye to the captain and to the other friends we had made on the ship and went ashore.

We went to see Kim and his mother, Valentina Petrovna, who welcomed us warmly. It was like coming home. We stayed with them for three days. We had promised the Commander's secretary to visit her and her opera-singer mother when we got back, so we went there one evening. We had the warmest reception from those wonderful people. We will always remember them in our hearts with gratitude.

Astrakhan was a beautiful Asiatic city. It had parks, exotic flowers and trees, and mosques. It was a hilly city with street cars going up and down. It was clean. It was like being on a honeymoon after our ordeals.

Living across the street from the railroad station, the station was like home to Kim. He knew everybody and everybody knew him. We went over to make arrangements for leaving Astrakhan to go north. We were all very heartbroken, - we felt like family. Valentina Petrovna came home from work to see us off. Kim cried like a baby. He stayed at my side the whole time, until the train departed.

We had to wait in the station because freight trains had priority with shipments to the front. After about three hours we left Astrakhan for our big journey. We headed north but we had only a vague travel plan, not knowing the war situation. All that was certain was that we were going toward the front lines to try to reach my brigade.

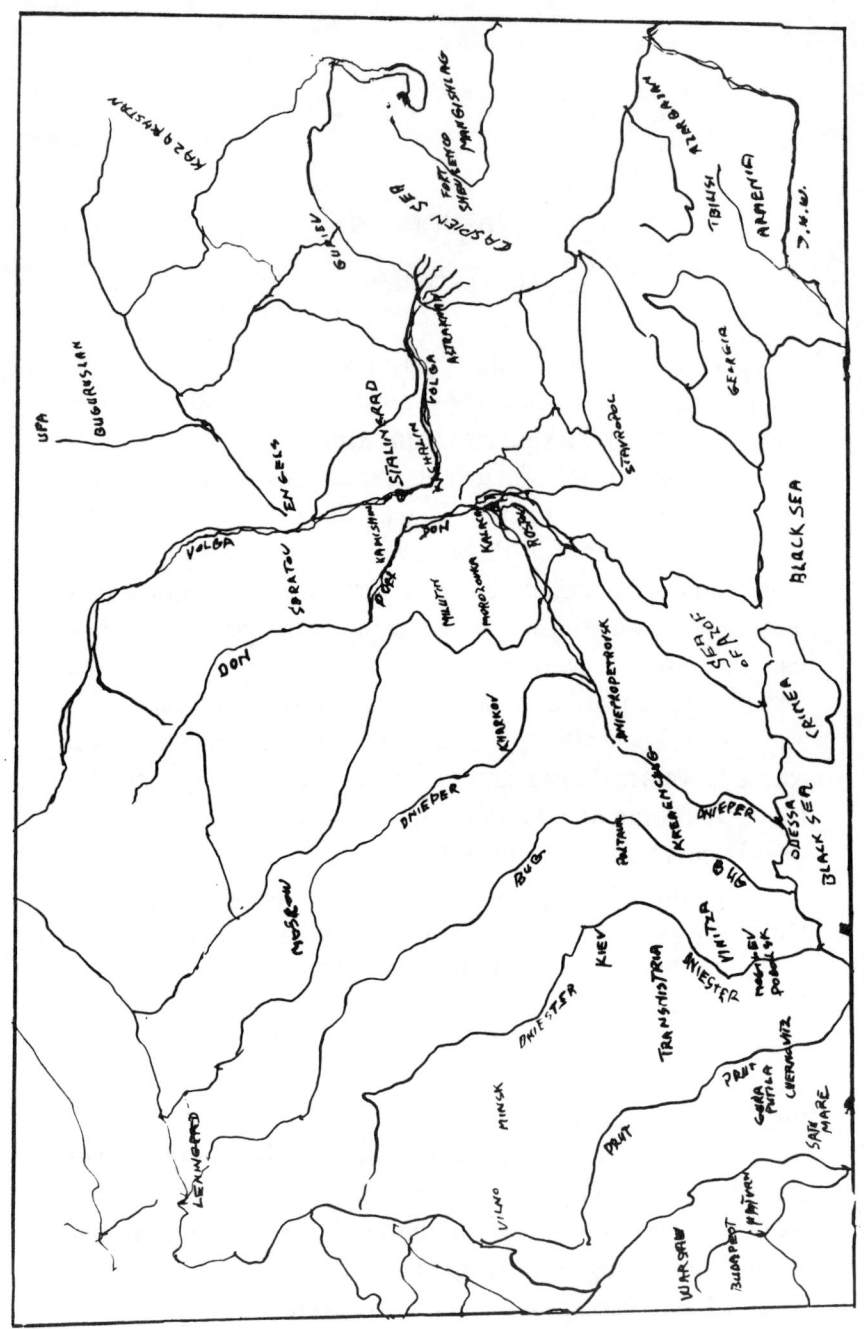

Chapter 15:
A Special Mission

On the way to the front, I had a special mission to fulfill. I had made a promise to my brigade commander, Vassil Yonovich. We had started out together in the Resistance and were good friends. He had been a civil engineer in the Ukraine.

His mother, wife, and three-year-old son were in a refugee camp in Ufa on the border of Siberia. He had asked me to go to see them, to bring them personal greetings, to give them money, and to look to their needs. My going there would be almost like his being there.

I knew that this would be a long trip and not an easy one. Gabriela and I decided to make our first stop in a remote town near Saratov, which is across the Volga from Stalingrad. We got off the train at Onishcsenko. I knew people there with whom we had been in contact during the fighting for Stalingrad. We used to go there for supplies from the collective farms.

I left Gabriela there with one of the families while I traveled further north to Ufa. We decided that my traveling alone would be much easier than with her. I had more chance of reaching my goal knowing that she was safe. I did not want to expose her to such hardship. I would have to sleep in railroad stations, change trains frequently, and do a lot of walking. She was not up to it physically.

After thirty-six hours of traveling I arrived in Ufa and went straight to the refugee camps, where I found my friend's family. They knew I was coming. Vassil Yonovich had written to them. I was able to give them sugar, vodka, smoked bacon, and other foods. I also had money for them. I stayed there overnight, and saw to it that they had everything that was in my power to do for them.

Then I traveled back to Gabriela. Arriving there, I really needed a rest. The week I was away had exhausted me.

While I rested we made our travel plans to try to reach my brigade. Gabriela said she would like to stop in Stalingrad to see a family that had helped her at the pier on the Volga River when she had passed through there.

Chapter 16:
Back To Stalingrad

In 1942, when Gabriela and her group of people were evacuated from Milutyn, they had stopped in Stalingrad in order to board ships that would transport them down the Volga to Astrakhan. They had to wait for almost two days in the open on the pier. They had no food, no water, no shelter. The war was in full force. Authorities could not pay attention to civilian refugees. Private citizens came out to the pier with bottles of water and crusts of bread and pieces of fruit to help the refugees. Gabriela sat in a corner with a woman who had a baby in her arms. In order to give the mother a chance to lie down and stretch out, Gabriela took the baby from her.

An elderly woman with a little boy and a young girl walked by. Seeing Gabriela holding a baby in her arms, they offered her some water and some fruits, and asked her how old the baby was. Gabriela said the baby was not hers and pointed out the mother of the baby, who came over and took the baby back. Gabriela gave the fruit and the water to the mother. The elderly woman was touched by Gabriela's readiness to help the mother. They asked if she was alone. They invited her to come with them to refresh herself. They lived very close by.

Gabriela thanked them but said she was afraid to leave because she was not sure when boarding would start. The young girl offered to stay on the pier and listen for the boarding announcement. The little boy said he would stay with his sister and would run back to the house to tell Gabriela when the announcement was made.

As it happened there was no boarding call and Gabriela was able to stay overnight. She got a bath, a bed to sleep in, and a hot meal. The children were up most of the night keeping watch at the pier for her.

So that is why Gabriela wanted to stop off in Stalingrad to find out how this family was and to thank them.

In the next few days we gathered supplies for the big trip to the front to try to reach my brigade.

We started out crossing the Volga River by ferry with Stalingrad as our destination. Transportation was still disorganized. The remains of the battle of Stalingrad were visible. The soil was still frozen in many places.

The city was deserted like a ghost town. The smell was terrible. There was no water or electricity, and the sewer system was completely destroyed. There were dead bodies covered with mud and ice. In many places they had started to pile them up into big mounds with tractors and ropes. Gasoline was being poured over the bodies which were then set on fire. Mass graves were also being dug.

We made our way into the city by freight train and by foot. Arriving in the city we could not believe our eyes. Those big buildings of that big, beautiful city were leveled down to the ground. We could not see one building standing up. Everything was flat like the palm of my hand. We walked around for hours to find the pier where Gabriela had met the family that helped her. From there we hoped to find the street and then the building where her friends lived.

It took us a long time to figure out where the apartment may have been. There was nobody around to ask. Everything was destroyed. We looked around through the ruins for a picture, a name, a sign of her friends. We could find nothing. We decided to write on a piece of board that we were here and stuck it into the ground. Maybe somebody from the family would come back and read that we had been there to thank them for their goodness and kindness to Gabriela.

This was the most horrible war scene we had experienced so far.

Suddenly we heard tramping feet. Down the street came a long line of unkempt, bedraggled Nazis being marched to prison camps by Russian soldiers. It gave us great satisfaction to witness this.

At the pier in Stalingrad, fall 1941 J. H. Wachtel

Chapter 17:
Return To The Brigade

We left Stalingrad and started towards the front. Hitching rides on military trucks was now easier. Railroad tracks were being repaired feverishly for supplying the front. The Nazis were retreating in desperation. They were running like rats.

We were unaware of what was happening to the Jews - that they were being exterminated in Babi Yar, Mogilev Podolsk, and other places in the Ukraine. We found out later as we passed through the Ukraine that the Jews had been annihilated by the Nazis.

In Kremenchug I heard for the first time about the massacre at Babi Yar. When I had fled the camp at Mogilev, it was the beginning of the war and these actions had not yet taken place.

As we traveled further we learned more and more. I now found out how to reach my unit, which was attached to the Second Ukrainian Front under the command of Marshal Malinovsky. All the resistance fighters and partisans had to be under some protection and command. We were given secret passwords for identification. The Jewish resistance fighters were highly regarded by the high command who knew we would never surrender or desert and would fight to the last breath.

After about two or three weeks traveling toward the front lines, Gabriela and I reached my brigade in the area of Kharkov in the Ukraine.

After a big reunion celebration and happy homecoming I walked away with Vassily Yonovich and we lay down on the grass. I started telling him about his family in Ufa - his son, his wife, his mother, - how they lived, how they looked, and the messages they sent him. With tears in his eyes he lay on his back, looking up into the sky, with his hands under his head. He cried and cried and I cried with him. Finally we were interrupted by others, who came to look for us.

Chapter 18:
The Nazi Retreat

My leg was improving day by day. Gabriela had a hard time adjusting to the nomadic life of resistance fighters. We were permanently on the move, sleeping in our clothes in barns, under trees, in horse-driven wagons, seldom in a house.

The front was moving fast. The Nazis were running in desperation, trying in some places to regroup and counter-attack, but never succeeding. We covered many miles in twenty-four hours, mileage that in the past would have taken us a week or two. From Kharkov we advanced towards Poltava. We stopped at the outskirts of Kremenchug and here we learned about the horrors of Babi Yar.

We tried to go there, but were not allowed by the local and military authorities. I was very much alarmed about the whole situation. I had left my family in Mogilev, which was on the same route.

We were told by the local people of the many atrocities committed by the Nazis during their retreat.

Our morale was very high, seeing the beaten enemy on the run. Stalingrad had completely demoralized them. Defeat had come to the arrogant blood-thirsty Nazis. What they had tried to inflict on others was now happening to them. We watched them run, barefoot, in underwear, trembling for their lives. This was the beginning of driving them back through the steppes and the woods and over the rivers of the Ukraine.

    Gabriela became slowly adjusted to our life on the front. She was assigned to our sanitation-medical group. In our brigade we had all kinds of sick people, not only those wounded in combat. Some had diarrhea, sore throats, colds, frostbite. We always tried to keep them in a safe place for two to three weeks, and then one of us would go with a truck or wagons to pick them up and bring them closer to us. We could not leave them behind in local hospitals for fear of losing them. We were like a family and meant to stay together.

Chapter 19:
Hardships Ahead

When the Russian army changed its tactics from defense to offense, it made a lot of changes in our way of life. Until Stalingrad the Russian army was in retreat and we along with them. We had had to avoid the rural countryside as well as populated areas for fear of being captured by the Nazis or by bands of their collaborators. We stayed mostly in the woods hiding, fighting, and running. Sometimes we didn't take off our clothing for weeks and even months. We were unshaved. Chances of cleaning and changing underwear were rare, even impossible. We were infested with all sorts of insects and parasites.

The cold winter was hard on all of us. We tried very hard to prepare for the cold weather, but in many instances had to leave behind all our possessions during an alarm or a retreat, especially such things as felt boots. These were called *walinkis*. They were boots made out of sheep wool that came up to the knee and were very important to avoid frostbite. We could sleep in them and they were comfortable and retained body heat and were usually waterproof. We did not have socks or shoes but wrapped our bare feet in rags (flannel if we could get it) specially cut to size and then pulled on the walinki. Even the regular combat soldiers in the Russian army used walinkis during the cold winters. It was well-known that if you were able to keep your feet dry and warm you could survive the biggest frost in winter.

By the time Gabriela and I caught up with my brigade, the Russian army was pursuing the Nazis and was well to the west of Stalingrad, even west of Kharkov. I had been reunited with Gabriela in March, 1943. It had taken me a year to locate and rescue her. It was in May, 1943 that I returned to my brigade with Gabriela.

To me this situation of pursuing and chasing the enemy was new. I had been away for almost three months from my brigade, and had to get acquainted with a new way of life. Having Gabriela with me, trying to protect her because she was still frail, changed my relations with some members of the brigade.

I had been tough and daring. I used to blow up convoys and derail trains and was respected as an aggressive and responsible member of our brigade. Now I started softening. I was concerned about Gabriela's health and well-being and tended to stay closer to her rather than being in the forefront of the activity.

Some of the brigade members were jealous of my having my wife with me. Only about half of the brigade were Jewish. Anti-semitism began showing up, especially after a drink or two. A drink was 90 proof vodka, an eight-ounce glass of vodka in one hand, and a glass of water in the other to wash it down. Vodka was more important sometimes than food. And for vodka you could get food. It was a trading item.

We were now in the Ukraine. We were passing through villages and collective farms free of the Nazis who had occupied them. The majority of the people in this area were deeply religious Christians. During the Nazi occupation they had been able to display their icons, which they had had to keep hidden under Stalin's rule. Most of the population were happy to be liberated from the Nazis, but some had mixed emotions.

We needed places to stay overnight, sometimes even for

a few days. We asked local homeowners to take us in, sometimes for money or by trading or by doing work for them. Sometimes we avoided mentioning that we were Jews because of local anti-Semitism. These were areas known for pogroms before the Revolution. We also felt the Nazi occupation had added to the anti-Semitic poison in the Ukraine. By now there were almost no Jewish inhabitants left in this area. They had either been killed or deported to concentration camps by the Nazis, or had been evacuated by the Russians and sent into the hinterlands of Siberia or Kazakhstan.

We also had the problem about being husband and wife. Almost all Russian men were at the front in the army. Some villagers would be jealous about our being together as a married couple, so in many instances we passed ourselves off as brother and sister or just friends in the same unit.

Even in our unit there was jealousy over things like our getting a better room, but gradually everyone grew to like Gabriela because she was like a sister to all of them.

The methods of fighting changed a lot in our brigade. The Russians started using us as an auxiliary working and maintenance unit, repairing roads, small bridges, and restoring buildings. In some instances we were sent ahead of the combat units to repair blown up bridges and roads. We also had to go into villages to organize local people to help transport lumber and stones by horse- and oxen-driven wagons. We had to convince the peasants that we were fighting for them and for the motherland even though we were in civilian clothes. This was the first time we were a liberating force working together with the Russian army.

Spring 1943, crossing the Dniepr 'Galia' broke the ice, was almost killed.

Chapter 20:
The Russian Rivers

All the big rivers of Russia run from north to south. Going west from Stalingrad they are the Volga, the Don, the Dnieper, the Bug, the and Dniester.

The rivers represented stumbling blocks for the Nazis during their advance as well as their retreat. The Volga River completely stopped their advance. They never crossed it and it was fatal to them. They were encircled in Stalingrad and suffered a complete defeat. From there they were driven back and had to cross the Don, the Dnieper, the Bug and the other rivers. As they crossed the rivers in retreat, they tried to blow up the roads and bridges behind them.

We were crossing the Dnieper in early May, 1943, when the spring thaw began. The river ice, which had been as much as ten to fifteen feet thick, began to melt and crack in some spots. Water was now visible in spots on the surface. We knew this was the last chance to cross the river.

Frozen rivers were the best means of transportation and communication. Crossing frozen rivers was ideal. Our brigade had a few trucks. We had picked them up from the fleeing Nazis and had repaired and maintained them until they needed spare parts or gasoline; they then became useless to us and had to be abandoned. Horse driven wagons and sleds were our best means of transportation. We even had spare horses and kept them almost as pets and used them only for horseback riding.

Our commander, Vassily Yonovich, had a mare, a beauty. Her name was Galia ("little dove" in Russian.) She was black, with a pretty little head and two beautiful ears and eyes. She had a white star on her forehead, and when she looked at you she seemed to be smiling. She walked as if she were on clouds. While riding her you had the feeling you were sitting in a rocking chair or in a cradle. We just loved her. She was never used for wagon duty, only for horseback riding and only a few people were permitted to ride her.

We started crossing the Dnieper. First a group of three people were sent to test the ice for safety and to set a marked path by forcing posts into the ice. The distance was about a half to three-quarters of a mile. All the sleds were put on the ice with light loads and were pulled and pushed by people. The fourteen horses were led with long ropes tied to their necks and waists and were handled by two or three people per horse. About half of the brigade had crossed safely with about seven horses, and we prepared for the next transport of two horses, Galia being one of them. Six people were leading the two horses with ropes. The men were about ten feet ahead of the horses, so as not to concentrate weight on the ice. The first horse crossed safely. After about fifty yards the three men leading Galia began to give signals of alarm. They called out, "The ice is breaking and cracking under Galia!" She also became alarmed at the cracking ice and started stumbling and dancing, trying to find stable footing. The people with her could not calm her down.

We rushed toward them and as we arrived there, she broke through. Only her head was visible above the ice. We all grabbed the ropes attached to her. Others brought blankets, spread them on the ice, and crawled on their bellies almost to her head. She looked at us with desperation. Her eyes were staring and begging us to save her. All of us were in great danger. We talked to her and she seemed to understand and cooperate. We begged her to try to put at least one foreleg on top of the ice. We all worked in turns more than an hour. The ice started to break off in pieces around her, and the more we pulled on her the greater the danger became.

Vassily Yonovich, seeing the situation, was fearful of a greater tragedy, that the ice breaking around Galia would prevent the rest of the brigade from crossing at all. He ordered us to leave her and retreat. He took out his gun, pointed at her head, and pulled the trigger. The gun did not go off. We all stood silent for a second, then as one cried out, "Don't shoot!"

We got down on our bellies again and feverishly started working on her. She also felt she must do more. With all of us working to the utmost, in about five minutes, she got both her forelegs on top of the ice. We started pulling at the ropes and we could even reach her saddle. In a few minutes more we worked her on top of the ice, lying down and trembling. We pulled her away from the hole. She was still motionless, as if she knew how to behave in this time of danger.

We dragged her on a blanket back to the shore. We helped her to get up. She was trembling from the excitement and the icy water. We made brushes from straw and rubbed her down for her blood to circulate and we even gave her vodka from a bottle. As she started to walk slowly and shakily, we proceeded to cross the river again, this time without incident.

Although Galia was rescued and made the crossing, she was never the same again.

Chapter 21:
Chasing The Enemy

The retreating Nazis left behind misery and devastation, especially in the rural areas. People were afraid of newcomers and strangers. All kinds of suspicious characters were roaming the area. Nazi soldiers and their collaborators were throwing away their uniforms and putting on civilian clothing to hide from the advancing Russian army.

It took us a long time to convince the local people that we were a special brigade attached to the liberating Russian army, especially since we were also in civilian clothing. We explained to them that we repaired roads and bridges. We were finally given shelter.

Very often we had to do work at night or go on extended missions. We sometimes were gone for days or weeks.

On one of my missions in the Ukraine, between Poltava and Cherkassy, heavy fighting was going on. We were caught in the middle between the river Sula and the Dnieper. I was completely recovered from my wounded leg and I was going on daring missions as before. I also wanted to prove myself to my unit. Now that Gabriela was safe, I was morally stronger, feeling her support, and thankful to God that I had been able to save her. I was happy to be able to fight for our people, to avenge the sufferings we had had to endure from the Nazis.

We did not know yet exactly what went on in the

concentration camps ahead of us in Transnistria, in Poland, in Auschwitz, Treblinka, and so on. We did not know those camps even existed. In the regions we passed we could see general destruction, but not what was happening to the Jewish people. In the Ukraine the Jews had either been evacuated by the Russians, or had fled on their own. Those who were left had been deported by the Nazis or eliminated on the spot. The civilian population was not generally aware of the Jewish plight.

Eleven of us were on a special assignment. We worked hard day and night for two or three days. We were dirty, tired, and hungry. Eight of the eleven were construction engineers. The rest of us were in charge of supplying and commandeering laborers, tools and materiel for the engineers. We also gathered local workers to transport lumber for telephone posts, bridges, and so on. We also asked for volunteers with horse- and ox-driven wagons to deliver the materials to the work areas.

In the town of Znamenka, near Cherkassy, we stopped for a rest in a collective farm. We asked for some food and water to wash up. There was not much food available. There certainly was no bread. The farm was almost deserted. The people were hiding in their homes. The office of the collective farm and the warehouse was attended by an old woman. She said to us, "They took everything!" And we realized the Nazis had taken or destroyed whatever they could. But she said she could give us water and could share with us what she had. She had some honey in jars and some sour pickles in barrels and invited us to help ourselves.

We also had some vodka with us and we sat down at the table. The woman put the honey into a large dish and the pickles in another. We were so hungry we dipped the pickles into the honey and stuffed ourselves. We washed it down with the vodka.

We thanked the woman for her hospitality and took off. We were about an hour's drive away when one of us started banging on the cab of the truck to stop. Everyone used the occasion to relieve himself. We then got back on the truck and in a little while, another bang and another stop. We all realized that the pickles and honey had hit us.

It took a long time to get back to our base. All of us were suffering from diarrhea and cramps. After a few hours we arrived. All eleven of us were very sick. Gabriela and the other women in the infirmary had their hands full. I, for instance, had dysentery. If Gabriela had not been with us who knows what would have happened. She nursed all of us. Every hour it got worse. In twenty-four hours I had lost so much body fluid and weight that she could carry me in her arms. Dysentery is very contagious. We had no medicines for it. We tried home remedies, like drinking powdered charcoal in water. The building we were in had only one outhouse. In order not to expose the people who owned the house, they tried to keep us away from the outhouse and they carried us to the back of the barns where they had dug holes in the ground. I was down to eighty-five or ninety pounds. If Gabriela had not been there I don't think we would have survived.

We were tended with such care, that in two or three weeks most of us started recuperating. Two or three had to go into the area hospital and we had to leave them behind.

Bakery shop, Mogilev-Podolsk 1943   J. H. Wachtel

Chapter 22:
Family Reunion

In June 1943 we advanced from the Bug to the Dniester River following the Nazis driven by the Russian army. We arrived at the Dniester and found that all the bridges had been blown up by the retreating Nazis. We were summoned to construct a crossing over the river. We helped set up pontoon bridges, which consisted of a line of boats or barrels covered with lumber of any kind, - planks, trees, electric poles -- whatever we could find -- to allow the Russian army to cross. At the same time we worked on repairing the blown-up bridges. I was kept so busy I did not get a chance to go to Mogilev Podolsk to hunt for my family, whom I knew to be in that area..

Every so often we met groups of people. They looked starved, their eyes were blank, they wore tattered clothes. Many seemed emotionally traumatized. We knew right away they were vicitims of the Nazis. We stopped and tried to help them with food and clothes. They had been liberated by the Russian army.

We crossed the Dniester only a few days behind the Nazis, and set up our camp in the woods near the river in the town of Soroka. A very exciting thing happened to me there.

Smoke and fire were everywhere. The Nazis had tried to blow up everything behind them: factories, schools, electric utilities, medical facilities, and so on.

Lev, one of the brigade members, was in charge of food supplies for our unit. One day he stopped his truck in front of a former bakery shop in Mogilev. He had come from our camp to look for supplies and to start up a bakery. He noticed a group of people who were obviously concentration camp survivors.

Lev spoke to them. "Where are you from?" he asked.

One of the men answered, "We are from the Mogilev Podolsk ghetto. The Russian army liberated us."

Lev asked, "How many people are still in the ghetto?"

The man answered, "Quite a few, but many are sick with typhus and other diseases and we have no medicine or doctors." Then the man added, "I'm a butcher. Maybe you can use me. I will work for you."

Lev asked his name. The man answered, "Mayer." The driver asked some more questions and finally said, "Okay, Mayer. I will see to it that you find work."

While they were talking, he asked Mayer if he had a family. Mayer said, "Yes, I have a wife, two little boys, two sisters, an aunt and her children. We are all there in the ghetto on the outskirts of Mogilev. We all stay in one big barrack. We sleep on the floor, on straw sacks covered with rags."

Lev asked, "Were there any others in your family?"

Mayer answered, "I had three brothers, one other sister, and my mother. We do not know where they are. My oldest brother was killed by the Nazis in the ghetto. My second brother disappeared during one of the deportations. My youngest brother was here in the camp with us but joined a group of young people who ran away to join the resistance."

With tears in his eyes, Mayer took out a mutilated little snapshot from his pocket and showed it to Lev. "This is my youngest brother," he said.

Lev looked and looked at the picture without saying a word, but getting paler and paler. His voice started trembling and he asked, "Is this your younger brother?" "Yes," said

Mayer. Mayer started getting suspicious and asked, "Please, tell me -- what is it? Do you know him? Is he alive?"

"Yes," said Lev. Mayer collapsed, almost fainting. Lev supported him.

Mayer asked, "Is his name Josef?" Lev answered, "Yes." Mayer continued, "Do you know anything about his wife?" Lev answered, "Yes, her name is Ella, she's blonde and she is with him."

It took a long time before Mayer could come to himself. He and Lev finally decided not to say anything to the family for fear of the effect of the shock.

Mayer and Lev decided to go back to the ghetto. Mayer told his family that he had to go with this man on a small trip of about forty kilometers to pick up some cattle for slaughter. He might be gone overnight because it could be too dangerous to drive back after dark. Mayer did not want to tell the others in his family that Josef and Gabriela were alive until he was absolutely sure.

Mayer went back to the truck and helped load things that Lev had procured and they took off. The trip was not too long, but it was dangerous. Pockets of enemy soldiers were still around. Lots of Nazis threw away their uniforms and put on civilian clothing. Lev had a very good nose for them. He picked them out from far away. He knew how they hid and how to find them, wherever they were.

They finally reached the woods near the Dniester River where my comrades and I were stationed. Once in camp, Lev asked for Josef the mechanic. The answer was, "He's out on a mission. He will be back in about two hours."

Lev reported to the commander that this man was Josef's brother. Mayer, in tears, begged the commander to take him to Josef's wife. They finally decided to take him to the infirmary where she worked with the sick and wounded.

Lev went into the infirmary and said to Gabriela, "You have a visitor." She came out, saw a man standing before her. He was trembling, in poor health, emaciated, in poor clothing, dirty, unshaven. But as soon as they came close to one another they recognized each other and fell into each other's arms. Mayer was very weak and had to sit down. Everyone around them stood silent, shaken by the events happening before them. All waited in excitement for my return.

When I arrived in the camp on horseback I was surprised when I was sent to the infirmary instead of reporting my mission. When I came into the infirmary I saw Gabriela and Lev with another man coming out of the infirmary. The man was dirty, unshaven, and looked weak. I thought this was another Jewish survivor who needed medical assistance. And then I recognized my brother!

We hugged and we cried and we trembled together. After a while he began telling us about the family. We talked through the night.

Mayer stayed overnight. The next day Mayer and I prepared for the trip back to Mogilev with Lev to meet the rest of the family. We loaded the truck with food and clothing and took off. I sat in the back of the truck.

When we arrived at Mogilev Podolsk parts of the city were still burning. We drove through the streets through the rubble of destroyed buildings and finally came to the ghetto.

The ghetto consisted of a section of the city surrounded by double walls of barbed wire. Non-Jews had been evacuated from the area, and all Jews from the surrounding areas - from Bukovina, Romania, Bessarabia, and parts of Poland - had been rounded up and concentrated in the ghetto. Since there were not enough houses, barracks had been built.

Now the main gate was open. We stopped in front of the gate to work out a plan to prepare the family for our meeting. They were living in one of the barracks. With shaky steps I went in. The room was dark, airless, and with twenty to thirty people living in one room, the smell was bad. There was one small table with three chairs in a corner of the room. No one was sitting there. Everybody stood around or sat on the floor on straw sacks.

First my older sister, Sarah, jumped up and ran to me screaming and crying, "Yosele, Yosele." The room became like a madhouse; one after the other hugged, cried, screamed until Mayer and Lev managed to calm them all down, pouring water on those who had fainted.

Gaining a measure of self-control, I looked around and counted silently those who were present. I discovered someone sitting in a corner alone, not moving. I asked, "Who is this?" There was no answer. I repeated the question and became suspicious, approaching the person. Her head was between her knees. I lifted her head with my hands and there was Aunt Goldie, my favorite aunt, Uncle Joshua's wife. I looked around and asked, "What is this with Aunt Goldie? What happened to her?" She just stared into my eyes. Not a word came out of her mouth. Her head returned to her knees.

Now they started talking about what had happened to her. They told me that the Nazis had raided the barracks every week, beating up people, separating the sick from the others. Those who were able were put to work cleaning latrines, digging graves, burying the dead in mass graves, and all kinds of other inhumane work.

Typhus was the main killer in the camp. Uncle Joshua was one of the victims. Those who were struck with typhus were condemned to death. They were just loaded into wagons and trucked off to mass graves; even those who were still half alive. They were covered with dirt layers and sometimes you could see the top layer moving, from the movement of the live bodies in the grave.

The day after Uncle Joshua was thrown into the mass grave, Aunt Goldie went out by herself. She sneaked out, and seeing the moving bodies she lost complete control of her mind. Everyday she went out, taking a candle with her and lit it at the graveside and sat there until she was picked up by some member of the family.

I went with her to the gravesite after hearing what happened. I will never forget that scene. In memory of the dead the surviving families made makeshift memorial lights. Since candles were unavailable they would scoop out a potato and fill it with any kind of fat, then cut up pieces of rags or threads or rope as a wick, and light it. So many lights were carried by mothers, wives, children, brothers, sisters, friends that the gravesite was a big circle of flickering fire.

I was so angry at the sight. I said to myself, "How could God let this happen?" I lifted up my automatic gun, aimed at the sky, and emptied the cartridge of bullets.

Uncle Joshua had practically raised me. We were eight children, and it was not easy for our mother, a widow. I was not even twelve when our father died.

Since that sight at the gravesite, whenever I see the flame of a candle, I remember the mass grave in Mogilev, Transnistria. My Aunt Goldie died about a year later. In my mind she is still carrying that flame in her hand. May her memory always be with us. May mankind, never again, experience and see what I saw that day at that mass grave in Mogilev Podolsk.

Chapter 23:
In Romania

After crossing the Dniester River where I found my family in the camps of Mogilev Podolsk, we advanced through Moldavia down to Jassi into Romania. Big battles were taking place in Jassi. The Nazis hoped to make a stand with the Romanian army in the fight against the Russians.

After heavy fighting the Germans were beaten and driven out. In Romania we felt at home. We both spoke the language. All our friends who spoke only Russian tried to be with us. Here we found more Jews, because Marshal Antonescu had not cooperated when Eichmann demanded that he turn over the Romanian Jews. The Romanians did not deport all the Jews, only those from the borders with Russia, Bukovina, and Bessarabia.

In the town of Bacau I met Jewish people and I found out that some of my friends from Chernovitz were there. One man mentioned the name of Carl Pomerantz, who was my childhood friend. We had grown up together and worked together. I asked the man to come with me and help me find Carl. I promised him that I would bring him back to his family.

It was night time, but I was anxious to see Carl. The city of Bacau had been liberated only two days ago. There were no lights in the streets. People were afraid to walk around in the dark. We walked a long distance and finally reached Carl's house. We banged on the window. The people inside were afraid, but as soon as we started yelling his name, he recognized my voice and he opened the window. I dragged Carl right out of the window and almost broke his neck. We hugged each other again and again.

Next morning we went to find food for him and his family and their neighbors. All the stores were empty. There was nothing to buy in town. Carl knew of a flour mill on the outskirts of the city and food warehouses and farm markets, but they were afraid to move through the city, which was still a war zone. I commandeered a horse and wagon and together we loaded it up with sacks of flour, potatoes, and vegetables and I dropped him with the food supplies at his home. I returned to my unit and told Gabriela the whole story.

From Bacau we crossed over the Carpathian mountains. We went through Sighet, Elie Wiesel's home town, towards Satu-Mare, Gabriela's home town. As we crossed the mountains and the woods, groups of Jewish men who had been hiding in the mountains started to come out as soon as they were convinced it was safe. The Nazis had been driven from the region a few days ago. A few of us were on horseback, accompanying the wagons loaded with the sick and our personal belongings.

Once I looked ahead and I saw that Gabriela's wagon had stopped and screaming was heard from that direction. I galloped over. I saw a few men hugging Gabriela and shouting. They were friends and neighbors of hers from Satu-Mare. They had been hiding in the woods, watching our wagon train. When they decided it was safe to come out, one of them saw Gabriela and recognized her. He couldn't believe his eyes. He shouted to the others, "Come on! Look who's here!"

She took all their bundles on her wagon. She walked with them and introduced them to me and the others. They were so proud to see her as one of their liberators.

In the town of Baia Mare we found more friends. The word spread around very fast that Gabriela, her husband, and their brigade were among those who had liberated the region. They told her that her best friend and classmate, Borgida Anna, was in town. Some of the people ran to tell Anna what happened. A crowd came to meet us as we approached Baia Mare. They offered us rest and shelter and to stay with them as long as we were in town. Anna's husband, a lawyer, had been appointed mayor of the town. We stayed there ten days, then went on to the Hungarian border.

Crossing the Carpathian Mountains into Baia Mare - Satu Mare 1944
J. H. Wachtel

Chapter 24:
Prisoners Of War

The Nazis were retreating at great speed. We crossed the border near Debrecen, Hungary. In some places the roads were smooth, but when we arrived at the river Tisa, there were big obstacles to overcome. The main bridges were blown up and pontoon bridges had to be built fast in order to enable the Russian army to cross and keep the Nazis from regrouping. We had an order to collect empty barrels and to transport them to the river. Some of the barrels we found were full of wine, which we emptied, some into our mouths. We used the railroad tracks and all means of transportation to get the barrels to the river.

At the railroad station at Debrecen a big transport of about 200 German prisoners of war arrived to be shipped further into Russia. We were told we could use some prisoners for loading the barrels on the train. Some of the barrels were the size of a room. As I went over to get a group of prisoners from the guards, I noticed a man in civilian clothes, looking frightened. I had the feeling that he was a Jew. I went over to him, asked him his name and other questions in German, but he did not answer. I did not speak Hungarian, and I asked in Yiddish, "Are you a Jew?" He still did not trust me. I told him I was Jewish and would do anything to help him. Then he opened up a little and tried to explain in broken

German that he and his friend had been grabbed by Russian guards in the street. They threw him and his friend among the Nazi prisoners because they had to make up a head count.

"No matter how hard we tried to explain that we were Jewish they would not believe us," he said. The Nazis were laughing and teasing them. I ran over to my superior who was in charge of the railroad station and told him the situation. He sent another man to take over my job so that I could help the two Jews.

I went into town to get identification cards for them. I then gave the Russian guard a bottle of vodka and asked for five more helpers, including the two Jews that I pointed out. I had to be careful not to arouse his suspicions.

I took the workers away from the station and left the three Nazis with my friend and took with me the two Jews, who were from Budapest, gave them the ID cards, some money, and a bottle of vodka. I put them on a truck with Russian soldiers heading for Debrecen. I explained to them how to protect themselves on the road. I brought the three prisoners back to the prison camp and gave the Russian guard another bottle of vodka and told him the five prisoners were returned. He took my word for it.

One of the Jews, whose name was Rosner, said if we were ever in Budapest we should try to find him. He gave me his address.

In January, 1945, we entered Budapest. I looked for Rosner and finally located him. He and his family had a tombstone factory. About a month later our brigade was ordered to erect a monument in Hatvan, a town near Budapest, as a memorial to the fallen Russian soldiers. Rosner helped us and this was my first experience with sculpture. Rosner later said he would never have survived being with the Nazi prisoners if I had not rescued him.

Chapter 25: Liberation Of Budapest

Budapest is divided by the Danube into two cities, Buda and Pest.

After bitter fighting, the Nazis took a stand and put up heavy resistance there. After crossing the river from Pest to Buda over the bridges, they blew up the bridges behind them. They dug themselves into the Buda hills and made it impossible for the Russian Army to approach the river or to cross.

It took the Russians a few days to break through. Using pontoon boats they landed on the island of Csapel in the Danube, about thirty-five to forty-five kilometers south of Budapest. From there they crossed over the river and took the Nazis by surprise from behind and forced them to retreat. And so all of Budapest was liberated.

The city was in shambles and chaos. People came out from hiding, uncertain about the situation. We were told that we might have to stay behind to help restore the area.

We set up our quarters in the outskirts of the city. It was an industrial district called Koebanya, which means "stone mine." Here we could have access to tools and machinery.

From there we were able to follow the orders given us by the Russian command. We cleared the roads and organized the civilians to assist us. This enabled us to communicate with the people of Budapest and to find out about the Jewish situation. We learned about the deportations, how Eichmann had ordered one million Hungarian Jews to the extermination camps.

The famous Budapest synagogue was not destroyed. A few of us went there, on Dohany Street. There we found out more. All the Jews who were still alive in the area (many had been saved by Raoul Wallenberg) came to the synagogue to find out what was going on. My friends and I loaded food on our truck every day - potatoes, flour, cooking oil, bread. We drove to the synagogue and distributed it among the Jews. Gabriela, who spoke Hungarian, came with us.

The hope and happiness we brought them in such a desperate situation is almost impossible to describe. People were hugging us and thanking us for what we were doing for them. They also begged us to help find family members lost and seperated during the Nazi selections.

Since we also had to perform our official brigade missions, we often went without sleep for twenty to twenty-four hours a day in order to help our fellow Jews.

One day we drove into the city of Budapest. There were no street lights or stop signs at intersections. On one of the intersections our truck stopped abruptly. We almost flew over the cab from the open back of the truck. Gabriela was in the cab next to the driver. She jumped out of the truck, ran to the sidewalk, embraced a woman and screamed, "Clara! Clara!"

It was Clara Klein, who had been her classmate and best friend. They had sat next to each other for years in school. All the traffic stopped until our truck pulled over to the curb and we all got out.

Clara fainted in Gabriela's arms. We had to ask for water and a chair for her. As soon as she recovered, she told us her story. She had been saved by Raoul Wallenberg. We took her with us on the truck, and drove her home. The next day we returned with food. She told us that Gabriela's mother had been in Budapest but had been deported to Auschwitz on the last transport. She also told us that Gabriela's aunt, Ethel

Ungar, was alive and had also been saved by Wallenberg.

During our stay in Budapest in January, 1945, we heard of the arrest of Raoul Wallenberg by the Russians. The rumor spread around very fast, especially in the Jewish sector around the synagogue. There was no other way of getting news except by rumor - there was no radio or newspaper.

Everyone was frightened because of this. We thought, "It's terrible that a man of his stature can be arrested and for what, for the good he has done for the Jews? Maybe that was the reason he was arrested." Many Hungarians were anti-Semitic and were happy to see him arrested for such a crime, saving Jews.

When I visited the Budapest synagogue again in 1992 it was being renovated and restored. On the grounds there is a mass grave holding the bodies of Jews who perished in the ghettos. A beautiful weeping willow made of brass stands over the grave. The leaves, that quiver in the wind, contain the names of those buried there.

Dedicating the Hatvan Monument, May 1, 1945

Chapter 26:
Building A Monument

After the Germans were driven out of Budapest, the Nazi war machine started crumbling. We were moved around from one place to another to make bridge and road repairs.

As I mentioned earlier, we were an engineering construction brigade. We had about twenty or twenty-five architects and engineers on active duty, almost all Jews. They were: Vassily Yonovich Maierovich, the Commander, Rabin, Drabkin, Kaganovits, Fichtenberg, Lev, Bonenko, Pikazin, Berklau, Schieber, and others. Everyone had a special assignment. I was in charge of providing construction materials and tools. Lev and Bonenko were assigned to food supply. Fichtenberg and Drabkin organized labor pools from local citizens. All our work orders came from the Russian army High Command. Our brigade Commander was summoned to receive the work orders.

One day, sometime in January, we received an order to erect a monument in Hatvan to commemorate the fallen Russian soldiers. Hatvan had the heaviest battles in the region and had suffered great losses. So the High Command ordered us to build this monument. Hatvan is on the border between Czechoslovakia and Hungary.

Hungary had lots of heavy industry. Among them was stonecarving for monuments, tombstones, and buildings. On the road to Budapest we saw lots of materials which could be useful for the monument. After a trip to Hatvan to select a site for the monument, Rabin and Yasha, Jewish architects in our brigade, presented a design. Blueprints were drawn up. We had our first meeting and decided on the stone to be used, black granite and marble. We also needed cement, construction iron, and other materials.

We called in all our friends, including Rosner. Through him we got addresses for stonecarvers and construction workers. It was not an easy task. People were afraid to come out to work. They had had bad experiences with the Nazis and the Russians were not pussycats either. Having survived up to now, with the war still not over, they did not want to get involved. We went around convincing people that we needed their help and cooperation to do the job.

Mothers, wives, and children cried and pleaded with us not to take their men away. We promised transportation, food, and pay but we had a hard time to get them to work.

Among the stonecarvers was one influential person named Antal, who was a union official, an older man of fifty or sixty. He was recommended by everyone we spoke to, especially Rosner. We went to his home to try to persuade him to work with us. Like the others, at first he was not enthusiastic. He showed us how one wall of his house had been hit by a shell and was broken away. How could he protect his family from the elements if he left them in this condition?

I promised to help him repair his house and took him with me in my truck to the brigade quarters. Three men and I loaded the truck with lumber and tools, and went back to his house and helped him repair it. In half a day we had his family snug for the winter. We also brought food and salt for his wife and children. There was no salt to be had in all Budapest, but where our brigade was quartered there was a huge warehouse filled with salt. As a result we were able to attract many workers by supplying them with salt and food.

Gabriela was invaluable because Hungarian was her

native language and she could communicate with the local workers. We set up two stone workshops in Budapest. We brought in big blocks of granite from different warehouses. All the equipment in the workshops had to be checked and adjusted. There were big stonecutting and polishing machines. Huge cranes lifted the large blocks of granite, each about four or five tons, and placed them on a platform. A steel blade about ten feet long and one foot high with diamond edges was set in a heavy-duty machine with a constant water flow. The stone was cut to the size and shape according to the blueprint. Polishing machinery was also installed. Hand carving was done with hammer and chisel. Soon we had people coming from all over looking for employment, more than we needed.

In Hatvan, meanwhile, preparatory work had begun for the foundation and pedestal. We supplied cement, reinforcing iron, and cement mixers. Yasha was supervising in Hatvan and Rabin was supervising in Budapest. I had to supply both sites with materials and tools. As soon as a stone was ready in Budapest I had to get it transported to Hatvan.

It took several months to complete the monument. The stone factories of Budapest, which had been idle before we came, were put into operation and remained in production after we left.

The monument in Hatvan, Hungary erected in 1945 revisited in 1992

Chapter 27:

The Monument Today

After returning in 1992 to Hungary and finding the monument intact I went to Hatvan City Hall to try to find someone who knew the history -- why it was left standing when all the other Russian monuments were toppled.

Everyone who worked in City Hall had been born after the war and knew nothing about it. I was referred to the library. They told me about a retired professor, Nemeti Gabor, a historian who handled the archives.

The library called him and when he heard I was one of those who built the monument and wanted to talk to him, he came running to the library and greeted me as an old friend. He took me to his office and showed me photos taken when the obelisk was dedicated, in 1945.

I asked him, "How is it this monument was not destroyed?" He answered, "Because some wise person added to the inscription the words 'and Hungary.'"

At that moment I remembered what had happened. We were sitting in the office of the Russian Commander getting the order for building the monument. A few Hungarian stonecutters were with us and my wife Gabriela was the interpreter.

When the Commander gave us the wording for the

inscription, "To always remember the heroes fallen in the battles against the Nazis for the freedom of the Soviet Union", Gabriela felt bad that Hungarian workers were involved and the monument would be in Hungary, yet Hungary was not mentioned. She suggested to the Russian Commander that the words "and Hungary" be added. He agreed, with a big smile, and the Hungarian stonecutters embraced her.

So now the inscription reads, "To always remember the heroes fallen in the battles against the Nazis for the freedom of the Soviet Union and Hungary."

After getting back to Budapest, the next day I went to look for the stoneyards where the obelisk was cut and polished. Sure enough, after a whole day of driving around the stonecutting area, I found one of the stoneyards still in operation, the old-fashioned way, exactly as it was forty-seven years ago!

Chapter 28:
The War Ends

In April, 1945, after finishing the monument, we were moved through Hungary and Czechoslovakia. We went through Brno, Pilsen, Prague. The winter was harsh, especially in the mountain regions. Fighting continued but our work had to be done to maintain and repair roads for the Russian troops. The Nazis put up heavy resistance in many places and even counterattacked.

We came closer to the Austrian border and to the communities of German-speaking people, such as Sudetenland. The roads were devastated by the retreating German army. These were unpaved side roads that were full of potholes and, in the melting snow, became mudtraps. Sometimes one foot would sink in, and by the time you freed it, the other leg would be trapped. We had to keep moving equipment and materiel. I was on horseback and was responsible for keeping our brigade moving. The wagon train was about half a mile long. The roads were narrow. Often the wheels of a wagon would get stuck in the mud and hold up the whole line until we could free it. Sometimes a wheel broke and we had to transfer the load to other wagons and abandon the vehicle. The horses and the men had heavy going.

In April we were on the outskirts of Brno, Czechoslovakia, restoring a small bridge which had been blown up by the retreating Nazis. We often worked at night to keep the Germans from knowing our project. We even tried to confuse them by having a dummy group making a lot of noise in a different location. One night in the middle of the job we got an order to leave immediately.

We were ordered to leave for Pilsen and Laa, at the Austrian border, not far from Vienna. We left Gabriela and the other medical workers behind in a small town near Brno to care for the wounded and the sick. We put in about a week of hard labor, restoring roads. Fighting was going on all around us. We had no rest and little food. We were unable to take time to get out of our clothes. We finally stopped for a rest in a wooded area near Laa and waited for daylight.

Suddenly we heard wild shooting. The sky was lit up by rockets. We could not understand what it meant. We were completely cut off from communication and decided to wait for daybreak to establish contact with the army units.

Just then an army platoon passed through the woods and we heard Russian voices. We approached them to find out what was going on. To our surprise, we saw them swinging rifles in the air, screaming, yelling, and drinking vodka. They shouted, "The war is over! The war is over! The Germans surrendered!" So we went berserk, too.

But then I stopped and thought to myself, "Wait a minute. But what about Gabriela? She and the others are a hundred kilometers away!" I asked the Commander, "What will happen to the others in Brno?"

It was May 9, 1945. I was given a truck and with three others in the brigade we took off for Brno. It was still nighttime. Driving back was very dangerous. We did not know what the situation was in Brno, whether they had heard the news. As daybreak approached we met many people - soldiers and civilians, running around yelling, crying, shooting in the air. The situation was chaotic. On the road back to Brno we saw some strange things. We saw Nazis throwing away their uniforms in the cornfields, hiding in haystacks and barns.

Some of them even shot at us. We decided not to chase after them but to make all speed to contact our infirmary near Brno.

After a very tense two- or three-hour drive, we reached our group. We loaded the sick and wounded and medical personnel on the truck and returned to Laa.

Gabriela told me they had heard the news at daybreak. When there was a lot of shooting, they did not dare to go out. She was very worried about us. And so we had another happy reunion.

Returning to Laa, we awaited further instructions from the Front Command, not knowing what to do next. We had thought the war would never end. Now that it had, we found ourselves in Austria, the land where Hitler was born.

Our feelings towards the Austrians were agitated: we were angry, bitter, and full of hate toward the people who had inflicted the atrocities on our people. Now that we had survived the war with all its horrors, how were we to act toward our enemy?

We knew we had to behave. We did not yet know the full story of Auschwitz, Buchenwald, and Treblinka. We knew we had to keep together, maintain our discipline, and stay organized until we returned to our homes. We were all from the same general area in Eastern Europe and Russia.

The whole brigade of about 150 stayed together until Budapest. There we began to break up very slowly. About fifteen of us were the commanding group, and we did not want to leave each other, and even talked about staying together forever.

On the road home we met all kinds of obstacles. The Russians treated us sometimes as second-class citizens. For instance we had to wait for transportation. We had no gasoline for the German trucks we had picked up and repaired. We seldom had rations for food. Now that the war was over the Russians stopped supplying us. We resented this treatment.

As Gabriela and I got closer to our home area, we almost did not know where home was. Was it Gabriela's home town, was it my home town? Where should we head for? Some wanted to go to the Ukraine, into Vinnitsa, or Kiev. Vassily Yonovich said, "Let's go to Siberia, to Ufa where my family is. We may be able to make a good living there. We can form a construction cooperative."

It took us a long time to decide to split up and disappear from each other's lives. There were many sleepless nights for all of us. We remembered the moments of danger, how we sacrificed for each other, ready to give our lives for one another.

We finally said goodbye and each one went his way. Vassily Yonovich, the Commander, went to Ufa in Siberia. Drobkin went to Kharkov, Kaganovich to Kiev, Rabin to Vinnitsa. Gabriela and I headed for her parents' home, with the hope we would find them.

After a long journey we reached Satu-Mare. We found out that her parents were no longer alive. Gabriela's mother had been killed in the gas chamber in Auschwitz. Her father disappeared and nothing was ever heard about him.

Gabriela had had a big family before the war. There had been thirty-five including her parents, aunts, uncles, and cousins. Only six survived.

We remained in Satu-Mare and tried to get in touch with my family in Chernovitz.

Chapter 29:
In Satu-Mare

I finally reached my family by phone and mail. I found out that after they had returned to Chernovitz from the concentration camps in Mogilev, they could not return to their homes. All their belongings had been looted and ransacked and destroyed. Windows and doors were broken or missing. Those apartments that were livable had been given to local Ukrainians who refused to get out. The authorities did nothing to help them get back their homes. Anti-Semitism was even worse than before the war. The Ukrainians had hoped no Jews would return and were surprised to see them.

Those that survived in my family were my mother; my brother Mayer, his wife Toni, his two sons Israel and Dov; my sister Sarah; my sister Esther and her husband and their daughter, Fannie; my sister Pepi with her husband and his mother; and my half-sister Jenny. My uncle Joshua's wife and two children also survived, making a total of thirteen who had no home.

The entire surviving family decided to leave Chernovitz for good. They crossed the border from the Ukraine into Romania. They settled temporarily in the small town of Siret. My brother Mayer came to see me in Satu-Mare. We decided to find homes for the whole family in Satu-Mare until we could all get to Israel.

We found five apartments for them. The local Jewish organization helped us get furniture and household items from empty Jewish homes. Many, Satu-Mare Jews did not survive the Holocaust. We also helped other Jewish families resettle as they returned.

Many Jews preferred being in Romania or Hungary rather than Russia because they felt it would be easier to cross borders to Israel.

I rented a big truck and went to Siret and brought my family to Satu-Mare and settled them in their new homes. We found jobs for them and they stayed for four years.

In 1950 my brother Mayer and his family were the first to leave for the new state of Israel. The rest left soon after, but Gabriela and I stayed in Satu-Mare until 1960, because our application was denied for ten years. Because Gabriela was a native of Satu-Mare, the local authorities wanted us to stay as examples to influence other Jews to remain in the country. As former partisans we were highly regarded.

In 1959 after a long period when no passports were issued to leave Romania, a rumor spread on Yom Kippur when we were all in synagogue, that everybody who applied today for a passport would be given one.

The authorities cynically thought that the Jews would not act on Yom Kippur.

We went over to Rabbi Deutsch asking for advice and we wondered what to do. The Rabbi agreed that despite the holiness of the day, all who wanted to should make out applications. He put me and Dr. Ari Katz, a lawyer, in charge to go with the group to see that no harm came to them. About 110 people came to the police courtyard. The captain was astonished to see so many people assembled and tried to talk us out of applying and to come back in smaller groups, but we decided to stay together.

We stayed in the courtyard the entire day, helping each other fill out the many papers and documents. It was late in the evening when we finally got done. We even signed up the Rabbi.

And that is how we finally got our passports, in 1960, to go to Israel.

We packed up all our things in a wooden box, which had to be a certain size and weight. We took the train through Hungary to Vienna. We stayed in Vienna a whole year.

Gabriela, 1948, three years after the liberation in Satu-Mare

Chapter 30:
In Vienna

We had planned to go to Israel. When our train arrived in Vienna we were met by a representative of the Israeli Sochnut, an immigration organization. The Sochnut took away our passports and documents and said we would be transported to a temporary shelter in the Korneiburg camps on the outskirts of Vienna.

Before arriving in Vienna I had contacted a friend who lived there, named Martin Frisch. He said, "Don't go to those camps. They were former Nazi camps." So I refused to go there. Martin took us straight to HIAS (the Hebrew Immigrant Aid Society), and they gave us temporary shelter in a hotel. Martin wanted us to come to his house but HIAS wanted us under their protection. I got all tangled up between the Israeli Sochnut, the Austrian police, and HIAS, which operated in Vienna to bring refugees to America. Meanwhile I had no passport or documents. After three days the Israeli Sochnut called us in and said, "Make up your mind. If you are not going to Israel we will return your documents and you are on your own." HIAS didn't want us unless we could get someone in the United States to guarantee $10,000. The Austrian police wanted our documents; otherwise they would have to detain us.

My friend Martin found out that Vienna had another

organization for refugees, the IRC, the International Rescue Committee. I went to see them. I met with Mr. Faust, the head of the IRC. I told him my situation, which he verified with HIAS. He then accepted us under IRC jurisdiction and we had no further problems with the police, the Sochnut, or HIAS. Our passports were returned to us. The IRC found us housing, gave us a weekly subsidy, bought us clothing, and found temporary jobs for Gabriela and me. Our son, Peter, was fourteen years old and was placed in an Austrian public school and also an American-run school.

We stayed in Vienna about a year. The IRC then gave us an American visa and airplane tickets. We came to the United States under the Russian quota, which at that time was open because very few Russians came to America then. But I almost lost my American visa in Vienna. It happened this way.

For the high holidays we needed special tickets to be able to attend services in the big synagogue in Vienna. A friend from Satu-Mare, Dr. George Silaghi, and I went to the Jewish Federation to get the tickets I had been promised. The doorman at the Federation, an Austrian, had been ordered not to allow anyone else in for tickets. I told him I had phoned and was told that Soviet refugees would be able to get tickets. The doorman insisted he would not let me in and he tried to close the door in my face. I pushed him back and he fell down. There was a lot of commotion and the police were called. I was arrested and taken to the police station. My friend (today he is a doctor in Maimonides Hospital in New York) ran after me and pleaded with the police to let me go, but they booked me. They had not yet fingerprinted me when my friend George went back to the Federation and pleaded with them and they convinced the doorman to withdraw his complaint. And so I was set free, and even received tickets to the synagogue. We decided not to tell our wives about the incident. If I had been fingerprinted, I would have been refused entry into the United States.

Later, in America, when George and I told our wives

about it, Gabriela gave me that special look and said, "Thank you for telling us now and not telling us then. It would have terrified us if we had known about it."

The author visiting his family in Israel in 1962. (l-r) Sisters Jennie, Pepi, Sarah and mother sitting in front.

Chapter 31:
Starting Life In America

Arriving in the United States in October 1962, we were met by the IRC representatives who took six or seven of us by a small van to a hotel in Manhattan in Harlem. I had forty-three dollars in my pocket. All the hotel inhabitants were people brought over by the IRC. The hotel manager was Mr. Fuhrman, a Russian Jew who spoke a beautiful Yiddish. We became very friendly from the moment we met. He liked our son, Peter, and had a son about the same age. We had a bedroom and a separate room for Peter. We had a small two-burner range and a small refrigerator and were able to prepare simple meals for ourselves. Mr. Fuhrman gave me a lot of instructions about shopping, learning to get about in New York City, and looking for work. He took a special interest in helping me to find a job.

The IRC invited us almost every week for a few hours' discussion to help us adjust and to advise us regarding jobs and permanent housing. But what Mr. Fuhrman did was more than they could have accomplished.

He made lists of areas where to go and look for jobs, what kind of subways to take, how to handle money. After a week he accompanied us to sign up Peter in George Washington High School, about five blocks from the hotel.

In another week Gabriela and I got temporary jobs. She

worked in a watchband factory in Queens and I started working in a knitting factory in Williamsburg, Brooklyn. I started sweeping floors, cleaning machines, passing materials to the workers. Neither one of us spoke one word of English. In those factories there were always some employees who spoke one of the languages we knew - Russian, Hungarian, Romanian, German, Yiddish. Our bosses did not have any of those languages, so we could only communicate with the workers who interpreted for us. My salary was $60 a week. Gabriela made $45. This included piecework she took home and all three of us worked till midnight helping her.

Although Gabriela had a license as physical therapist and cosmetologist from Europe she could not practice until she had enough language to take the New York license examination. She took it two or three years later and passed it. She then worked at Interfaith Hospital in Queens for eight years.

Meanwhile we had to find an apartment. We had friends in Queens so we settled there. We had to pay $127 a month for rent. The IRC paid our rent for three months. Peter transferred to Forest Hills High School from which he later graduated.

After a few months I felt I knew enough English to look for a job in my specialty. In Chernovitz and in Cluj, Romania, I had been a textile and tricotage mechanic. We assembled the machinery that wove the material, like doubleknits and all kinds of fabrics for the fashion industry.

I got my first job as mechanic through one of Gabriela's cousins whose friend was a clothing manufacturer, Carpy Knitting and Fashions. I started with $110 a week, which kept increasing through the years.

One day I was approached by a jobber who had his own company and wanted me as a partner. I accepted his offer and we did a good business producing doubleknits which were then very much in demand. Gabriela left the hospital and came in with us to take care of the books. Peter graduated from high school and went to Pratt Institute in Brooklyn. He graduated as a chemistry major and took a job with Monsanto as a research chemist in Springfield, Massachusetts.

My partner, Joe Hammer, and I worked together for seven years. When he retired it was too much for me to handle alone. I liquidated the business and took a job as quality controller for a big manufacturer of ladies' sportswear for a number of years until I retired and moved to Florida.

The author's son Peter, Noemy, Natanya, Felice and Gabriela in their home in Florida

The sculpture in alabaster by the author, titled "Flame of Freedom" in the permanent collection of the Holocaust Museum in Washington, D.C.

Chapter 32:
In Florida

When my son Peter was a high school student he discovered an ability of mine. When he came home with art homework he would ask for my help. The next day he would come in from school and say, "Tata, you got yourself an A today."

Peter was so impressed with my art ability that he signed me up for an art correspondence course. I started learning how to draw and design and paint according to their instructions.

After settling in Florida I enrolled in art classes at the Norton Gallery Art School. When I took a sculpture class with Luis Montoya, and began chipping stone with the hammer and chisel, it became the most satisfying thing I had ever done. I began thinking of Hatvan, Hungary, and the monument we had constructed for the fallen Russian soldiers. I remembered the cutting of the stone and polishing it. And then I began to want to tell the story of the Holocaust in stone. The piece I created was "The Flame of Freedom" which represented for me the flames at the mass grave in the Ukraine where my aunt lost her mind. This sculpture has been donated to the National Holocaust Museum in Washington, D.C. Later I sculpted "Shoah", a 180 pound alabaster marble depicting the victims of the Holocaust and honoring those who fought back. I donated this piece to Temple Beth Tikvah in Lake Worth,

Florida in honor of the fiftieth anniversary of Gabriela and myself. Another sculpture, "Grieving Mother", cast in bronze, is now in the Yad Vashem Museum in Jerusalem.

Today I do my sculpture at Palm Beach Community College. It is like having my own studio.

Peter is married to a lovely wife and has two wonderful daughters. They live in New Jersey. He has a doctorate and owns a chemical laboratory. My latest piece of sculpture was commissioned by my granddaughters, Natanya and Felice, to create their cat, Sandy, out of pink marble.

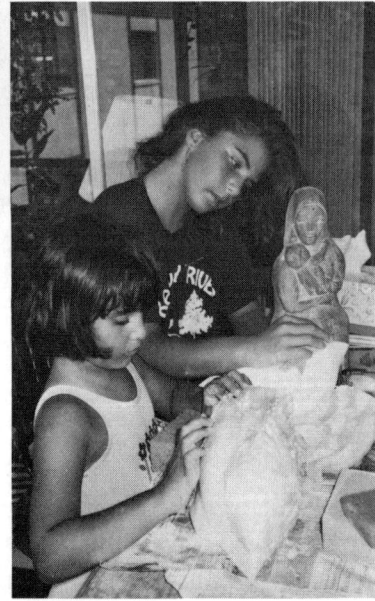

Above, Natanya & grandfather at Community College, Palm Beach, FL. Right, Natanya and Felice polishing his works.

Chapter 33:
Memories That Will
Live On Forever

Gabriela loved Florida very much. Many times she said, "These are the happiest days of my life."

We did so many wonderful things together, took trips abroad, made good friends, after sharing lives of danger and happiness.

In December, 1990, Gabriela became ill. We did not realize how serious it was until some time in January, when we learned that she had terminal cancer. On April 7 Gabriela died.

Today, a year later, she is very much with me, and will be with me forever. Our beautiful memories will keep me going and doing what she always wanted me to do. She was always the driving force behind me from the earliest days of our life together to the day she died. May she rest in peace.

Two weeks ago my granddaughters called me and said, "Tata, it is time to go to work and finish Sandy for us." So I went back to the college to work on Sandy, the cat, and get on with my life.

Above, "Grieving Mother" on permanent display in Tranistria Pavilion, Yad Vashem. Below, Yitzchak Mais, Director of Yad Vashem and myself at the dedication in 1991.

Epilogue:
The Grieving Mother

The sculpture, "The Grieving Mother", made of marble and later cast in bronze, I consider my greatest fulfillment and it has given me the most satisfaction since I have been creating art. This sculpture represents both our mothers as well as all mothers who perished in the Holocaust.

As the years passed by, during years of war, deportation, ghettos, concentration camps, fleeing, laboring in coal mines, collective farms, chasing the Nazis, fighting back - during those years, Gabriela always said, when we were together, "My mother would have loved you very much."

I always tried to envision Gabriela's mother Pepi, who would have loved me so much, as much as her own daughter. What did she look like? Through the ashes and fire I saw her face. A small snapshot was all we had of her.

Many years later I started working on a piece of marble. I studied the stone to decide what form it would take. I wanted to make a sculpture about our mothers, Pepi and Shaindel. I was looking for a face. I couldn't see one. I was looking for eyes. No. I could feel them, just an indication. An opening in her chest. An emptiness in her heart in the form of a question mark, Why? Why did all this have to happen to me and to my children?

The answer to "Why?" is in our hands, those who

survived the horrors of the Holocaust. If we forget and do not remember and do not tell what we saw happening it may happen again.

Mother Pepi perished in Auschwitz. My mother, Shaindel, survived, saved by righteous gentile neighbors who took her in as their aunt. She was blinded with cataracts in both eyes, and was confined to a room for four years. After the war we operated on one of her eyes. She saw again, left for Israel with one of my sisters and later died there in 1964.

"The Grieving Mother" now is on permanent display in Yad Vashem in Jerusalem, in the Transnistria Pavilion. It bears a plaque dedicated to the memory of Gabriela.